BUSHEL AND A PECK

HOPE, HEALING, AND UNCONDITIONAL LOVE...A MEMOIR

KAREN MALENA

D1221960

Copyright © 2020 by Karen Malena

All rights reserved.

No part of this book may be reproduced in any form or by any electronic or mechanical means, including information storage and retrieval systems, without written permission from the author, except for the use of brief quotations in a book review.

ISBN: 978-1-944938-30-7

VeroCasa Press

A division of AIW Press

DEDICATION

For Elizabeth and Elena. May your own stories be a blessing to others.

ACKNOWLEDGMENTS

So many people are responsible for the writing of a new novel. I'd like to thank my publisher, Michele Jones at AIW Press, editor, Alicia Stankay, graphic designer, Amber Custer, and extra special thank you to artist, Jessica Reinicke Griffin for the lovely drawing of my parents for the cover. I would also like to give applause to my beta readers, Vincent Alessi , author Lee Kricher, and author Susan Landeis.

As always, a special thank you to my husband Jim, son, Matt, and brother, Rick for their encouragement and support, AlzAuthors for giving me the courage to share such a personal story as many of them have done. My old writer's group, Pittsburgh East Scribes for their guidance through the years, and our beloved mentor, Mark Venturini.

Mostly I want to thank God for my family—a family who went through times of hell, but got many glimpses of Heaven.

PRAISE FOR OTHER BOOKS BY KAREN

Reflections From My Mother's Kitchen

Thank you so much for your book. I started on the plane and just finished it a few minutes ago. I enjoyed it so much.

I can't wait to read all of your books. I loved this one.

Be well, be happy, and keep on writing! Lots of love.

Mary Badham (Scout, *To Kill a Mockingbird*)

Sound of Silence

Have you seen *Equilibrium* with Christian Bale? I thought about that movie all the time when I read K. Malena's *Sound of Silence.*

But whereas *Equilibrium* deals with a man who tries to overthrow the system in a future where feelings are illegal, *Sound of Silence* is set in a world in which no one is allowed to speak. Malena's writing flows effortlessly and makes even a dark, daring subject such as this one entertaining.

Vanessa Morgan, author and screenwriter of *The Strangers Outside, A Good Man,* and *Next to Her* which have become movies.

Piggy

Editorial Review

Reviewed By Jane Finch for Readers' Favorite

Piggy by Karen Malena is a delightful story involving a cat and a mouse and their unusual friendship. Goober, a mother cat, has an adopted kitten,Peanut, and she entertains him by telling him the story of Piggy the cat and a mouse named Melvin. The story involves an assortment of other animals and takes the reader on a journey into the animal world. In a clever twist, Peanut finds out that the story his mother is telling him has far more meaning than he expected, and that someone close to him is involved in a way he had not imagined. The idea of the mother cat soothing her restless kitten with a story is charming, and the story itself is captivating.

This is a clever story that, although probably aimed at middle-grade age, would be lovely read to a younger child by a parent. I also think older children and even adults would enjoy the story and the antics of the animals. The author, Karen Malena, has done a really good job of weaving in a few life lessons. The fact that a cat and a mouse can be friends shows the importance of friendships and helping one another, even though the perception would be that they would be enemies. This is a gentle book with a story that is fun and enjoyable and also an exciting adventure. It's also about caring for one another and not always taking things on face value. I think it would make a perfect bedtime story where the reader could explain the story and its interpretations to a younger child.

ALSO BY KAREN MALENA

Other books by Karen:

With a vivid imagination, the lessons learned in childhood, and the love of a close, Italian family, Karen began writing heartfelt, inspirational fiction novels, one which closely follows many of the conversations she and her mother shared through the years: *Reflections From my Mother's Kitchen: A Journey of Healing and Hope.*

When her mother began showing signs of Alzheimer's- type- dementia in the last several years, Karen once again stepped into the role of caregiver for her aging parents along with the help of a wonderful brother. It was watching the love between her parents into the golden years which inspired her fiction novels about dementia: *Love Woven in Time,* **and** *Love Finds a Way.*

She has written several other books, *Piggy,* a fun cat story which showcases friendship and carries an anti-bullying message, and *Sound of Silence,* a cautionary dystopian tale about a society forbidden to utter the spoken word. Karen also is part of an anthology about rescue cats, entitled *Rescued Two: The Healing Stories of Twelve Cats Through Their Eyes.*

She blogs at *The Finch's Nest:* karenmalena.blogspot.com, and has a website, karenmalena.com. You can also find her on Twitter, Instagram, Pinterest, Goodreads, and Facebook.

INTRODUCTION

Writing a memoir is deeply personal. No two are alike as no two lives are the same. I'd like to think that the story that follows is not only about my mother's journey into dementia; it's so much more. It's the tale of two people who cared enough to take their wedding vows seriously and their promises to love one another until death would part them.

It's a story of sadness and laughter; darkness and light; despair and hope.

We couldn't have gotten through any of it without God's help. I'd like to think that we found a stronger relationship with Him through every trial we experienced.

I'd like to bring your attention to the ragged butterfly on the cover. It was very special to me for several reasons. Firstly, all butterflies were such a big part of my mother's life. She adored them and told a little story about "her special butterfly" that you will read in this book. Secondly, this particular butterfly reminds me of Mom: Broken, battered, and yet beautiful and thriving. May we all come to experience beauty out of our trials.

CHAPTER 1

Who are you? The mother asks her daughter.
The daughter, just a little girl, but already so grown up, wonders: why
doesn't she know me?
I'm the Virgin Mary, the mother says.

The scars on my mother's wrists, the reminders of her failed attempt at suicide many years ago, had faded much like her life. Her scalp showed through the wiry thin gray hair. Eyes once so sparkly blue seemed dimmer somehow, just like the way Mom appeared to me, fragile and almost transparent. For my mother seemed almost shimmery—there and not there at the same time. Her eyes were fixed staring up into the corner of the room she shared with another woman at the care facility.

My husband Jim sat quietly in a chair while I held her face so wrinkly and so loved between my hands.

"I love you a bushel and a peck. A bushel and a peck and a hug around the neck," I sang softly, my voice cracking with the tears that threatened. "Remember, Mom? You used to sing this to me."

1

She took a breath inward, her eyes straight ahead and up. As she exhaled, I heard it: The gurgle of the death rattle. A sound I'd read about in all the books on death and dying. It seemed an innocent sound at first. But I'd heard that particular sound once before with her many years ago. I'd heard it loud and long and it had terrified me.

"A hug around the neck and a barrel and a squeeze . . ." my voice broke in the middle of the song. Tears, long held at bay, began flowing. Sobs broke free from my chest and I let go of her dear face. I had to turn away.

Mom's roommate piped up then from behind the curtain that separated them. "Could you change the channel for me, honey?" And then, "Why didn't I get any dessert for lunch?" I wanted to scream. *Can't you see my mother is dying?* But years of polite upbringing by the woman who was slipping away little by little came back to me.

"Here, let me help you," I said.

My husband looked at me as if I'd lost my mind. I shook my head. *It's okay,* I mouthed.

While I searched for the roommate's television remote, my head swam with the realization that I'd soon be losing Mom. Only nine months before, we had said goodbye to my father, my mother's soul mate and husband of over sixty years. Even through dementia, she still mourned him. Dad, our rock and strength—the miracle man—the hero of our family's long journey. My brother and I missed him with an ache so fierce that it was difficult to talk about. How would we get through another death so soon?

I can't do this, Lord. I'm too weak. Is there any way I can bargain with you? Can you let this cup pass?

The roommate thanked me for helping her, and I walked back over to the other side of the room. Jim stood by my mother and spoke jokingly to her, as if this would snap her out of the state she was in.

I bent down and laid my head on my mother's shoulder. It was foreign, something I don't ever remember doing. Our family hadn't been affectionate and I wished that it could have been different. Here, at the end of Mom's life, I could show affection freely. *Oh Mom.*

Two days later, I stood in front of a casket once again. I laid my head upon the shoulder of my mother for the last time.

Our most recent journey with Mom started in about 2008. Dementia, the sneaky thief slowly began stealing my mother's mind, replacing it with simple conversations and yet oddly leaving a few precious memories of times past.

I knew I was fortunate to still have my mother during the beginning of her memory loss, but it didn't feel like her. It felt like a shell of who she once was. Conversations were replaced with questions, so many questions. We replayed past moments again and again. It hit me how childlike she had become.

Sometimes I felt as if all the good years in between never happened. This wasn't the strong woman who once ran several businesses of her own.

This wasn't the first time that Mom had issues with her mind. My own memories from long ago peppered my brain like the sting of tiny wasps. Emotions ran through me in succession: shame, fear, and anger. *It's happening again. It's not fair, Lord! I was a little girl, only a child.* The words, a litany of the small girl I'd once been, afraid as her mother was taken from her; a little girl who'd been lost and alone due to the descending darkness of her mother's mental illness. I wiped at the tears, overcome with emotion.

Nobody had ever given me a complete diagnosis of Mom's mental state. I'd only heard snippets of cruel words from insensitive people: depressed, crazy, suicidal. While growing up I watched as my mother returned home from hospital visits, a haunted look on her face and the smudges of dark circles beneath her eyes.

All that I'd seen, the spiraling depression and secretive whispering, threatened to pull me down. I became a nervous, hyperventilating child, preferring to retreat into the fantasy world of books and movies, making up my own tales where everyone lived happily ever after and mothers didn't talk crazy. Sadness and fear became constant companions and it was difficult to talk about my feelings. I daydreamed about having a normal family, but at times, I thought I might never see my mother again.

For the second time in my life, Mom was leaving me; but this time it was the memory thief.

CHAPTER 2

Several years ago, Mom got an invitation to join some ladies she graduated with from Ambridge High for a little social evening. I was thrilled because my mother didn't have many friends throughout the years. She was a little computer savvy and played games in online chat rooms, but that wasn't the same. To have ladies who were her peers reaching out to her meant something to me. Mom said she was always an introvert when she'd been in school. These seemed to be some of the "popular girls" and we all pushed her to go.

Dad was especially thrilled because though they were in their seventies, he still loved my mom with his whole heart. It brought him joy to see her happy. Mom got a cute wig to wear, and a new outfit. Dad drove her to the event and told her he would be back in about two hours.

I couldn't wait to chat with my mother on the phone the next day to see how the evening had gone. I knew it would be a smashing success and she would want to go again on their next outing.

"How was your night out?" I asked Mom.

"I didn't like it," she answered.

My heart sunk. "Why?"

"I think those ladies were talking about me behind my back."

How odd, I thought. Why invite her if they were going to act like a bunch of petty school-aged girls?

"Mom, seriously. . . I can't imagine that's true."

"Well it is!" she snapped. "I'm not going back."

When I visited my parents on the weekend, I went into my father's little craft room—the place he spent many happy hours blissfully alone. I lowered my voice. "What do you think really happened?" I asked.

Dad held two pieces of wood together as a string of hot glue dangled from one of them.

"Ah, she's nuts," he said. "She's been saying that about the ladies down the block, too, when we're sitting on the porch. Says they're talking about her."

I would have never said that Mom was paranoid. She'd become an outspoken woman with a big, compassionate heart. She'd been a business woman for several years, and I'd never felt an iota of insecurity from her during that time. I sometimes wondered about my own insecurity because I'd not gotten it from her.

"That's a shame," I said. I sat on the edge of the small sofa in the craft room. Surrounding Dad were metal coffee cans filled with nuts, bolts, pieces of wood and metal. Glass jars lined the windowsills that were filled with paintbrushes in an array of sizes. Other containers held precious dried flower seeds and strips of sandpaper.

Several handmade dollhouses with windows that opened and closed sat on a few small card tables in the room. Some had beautiful ornate wooden doors and homemade fireplaces. Others had elaborate wrap-around porches and faux bricks covering the exterior. Nature puzzles of birds and gorgeous scenery hung on the walls. Balsa wood airplanes hung from the ceiling in colorful World War II array.

Though I lost myself for a few minutes of peace in my father's special craft world, I knew I would have to face Mom again.

"I can't get this damn computer to work," Mom said throwing her hands up in surrender when I walked back into the living room. "I think your brother is messing with it again."

"Ma, Rick has his own computer. He doesn't touch yours."

"Oh yes he does!" her voice got louder. "I know he was on it. He stole my eBay site."

I closed my eyes and held my breath for a second. Who was this grumpy mother that disagreed with everything recently?

"I'm tired of cooking." Mom said next.

"I can make something," I said. "Or buy you guys a sandwich from a restaurant if you want."

Mom ignored me and grabbed her wooden cane, strolling out of the living room as fast as she could and next I heard cupboards banging in the kitchen and pots and pans crashing.

Dad appeared then. "Hon, what are you doing?"

"I'm gonna start dinner," Mom said, pulling a completely frozen hunk of meat from the freezer.

"We have leftovers," Dad tried.

"Gosh dammit, I want to make something."

And so it went. 2008 began with a bang of an angry woman. That is when we knew Mom was not the same.

CHAPTER 3

*A*nger turned into forgetfulness and so little of it at first that it was easy to dismiss. Aging people always forget something, right? As Mom began telling the same stories and asking the same questions, however, our family wondered if it might be dementia.

She started to pull out paperwork and read it as if seeing it for the first time. She went through her wallet and bank cards, health card, and license asking about each one as if she didn't recognize them.

Her cooking and baking suffered. Mom did her best work in the kitchen. It was where the magic happened; delicious meals and wonderful home-baked goods. Now ingredients were left out of recipes causing them to fail. None of us had the heart to mention it to her. I threw away food when she wasn't looking and felt guilty for doing so.

Movies were always such a big part of our family. Mom and Dad owned several DVD's of old favorites, and though we watched some of them many times through the years, my mother began watching her most-loved movie, *To Kill a Mockingbird*, several times a week.

"Wow," she said one day when I visited. "I must have seen this movie at least five times."

I looked over at my brother who had also stopped over that day.

Under my breath I added, "Yeah, five times one hundred." And it became a little joke between us.

Then Mom didn't want to watch her movie alone. If my father went into his craft room, she would call out to him to sit with her. Poor Dad patiently put down his little doll furniture and sat beside Mom as that same movie played once more.

I wanted to scream. *This is not fair to Dad! Let the poor guy do what he wants.* But my father was a peacemaker, the strong, silent type. And whatever was good for Mom was good for him.

My brother and I worried about our father. Around 1999, he had quadruple heart bypass surgery. He suffered bouts of congestive heart failure from time to time. Since Dad was such a giving soul, we wanted his quality of life to be filled with precious things that he enjoyed. It seemed that the worse our mother got with memory issues, the more Dad gave of himself.

My brother didn't live with them, but every night he drove to their house to sleep over on a small pull-out sofa in case they had an emergency. I was on the phone daily with my father helping coordinate doctor appointments for him or Mom. Life certainly was taking a different turn. From then on, it would never be the same. Our lives would become filled with our parents' tasks.

Dad asked me to take over the bill paying. Mom forgot to cook, and I'd make foods or buy some things for them to eat for a few days. Yet they still enjoyed a few simple pleasures together and it made my heart light.

Mom loved to take a short drive to the next town. Dad parked on a little stone bridge in the woods and they rolled their windows down to watch a small creek flowing and listen to the trickle of water. He often bought her a jelly donut to enjoy on these small excursions.

What they took most pleasure was watching birds and butterflies from their own front porch. Dad had installed a small pond and fountain in their yard. He brought out stale bread so that Mom could throw it into the yard for the birds. He grew colorful zinnias and marigolds which attracted all sorts of beautiful butterflies for her to watch. They always held a special meaning for my mother.

She told a story that once when she was despairing and sadness had overwhelmed her, she was at the sink looking out into the back yard. She begged God for a sign to know that He was there.

Mom said that the most glorious Monarch butterfly flew to the window right at that moment and almost appeared to be dancing as it fluttered just for her. It stayed for the longest time and she knew God had sent it. It was a story she never forgot and told often.

My parents also had a hummingbird feeder hanging nearby and the little birds would fly right up to their faces as they sat outside as if wondering who they were. Buzz, dart, drink, and buzz away again. Deep greens, royal blues, and sunshiny yellow buzzing beauties. Mom and Dad adored them. And they adored their outdoor time together.

It even appeared to me that their love grew stronger. They were approaching their sixtieth wedding anniversary—the true epitome of a good marriage. Little did we know that great loss was just around the corner.

CHAPTER 4

I was born in 1960. My brother didn't come along until fourteen years later, but my mother had two miscarriages between us. I often wondered what it would have been like if those babies had lived. How much different things would have been to have the support of two more siblings.

I remember that it had almost sent my mother over the edge, losing two babies very close together when I was a little girl. She'd hemorrhaged so badly during one that she had to be taken to the hospital. My Nonna—the Italian grandmother that lived next door to where I grew up—had come over to our house when it happened. I was rushed outside, yet later I thought I saw a towel bundled up that she was trying to hide. I watched the events unfolding feeling utterly alone and frightened. What were they doing?

All of a sudden death was all around. My mother's beloved sister, Clara, had become sick. She was only in her late thirties, but it was a devastating illness.

Mom and Aunt Clara laughed together on the phone all the time. Our family's visits were always fun. Though my cousins were a bit older, we were as close as siblings. Dad and Uncle Lou, Aunt Clara's husband, got along well. My uncle especially loved to rib my mother in a good-hearted way. Talk and laughter was always lively and loud when they came over our house.

At the heart of every Italian home is the kitchen. We all sat around the table while Mom put out plates of cold cuts, cheeses, sliced tomatoes, and soft bread. If nobody was eating, my mother gave them the eye. Everyone ate. Then the stories started and Mom began with her infectious laughter. By the time we were all done laughing, our sides hurt and it was difficult to catch a breath.

My mother adored her sister though they weren't that close in age. Clara was the one constant during their turbulent time growing up with an alcoholic father. My grandpap had not been an easy man. A gambler, violent and drunken, he would beat his wife while the children were nearby. My mother felt love from her sister that neither her mother nor father could provide. She'd been told from an early age that she was an accidental baby, a mistake.

When Aunt Clara was dying during Easter when I was eight years old, it appeared to rip sanity from my mother, leaving a shell of who she was. Almost overnight, constant anxiety surrounded her. Depression shrouded her and it felt as if the sunshine had gone out of the world. Though my mother had never been overly religious, she talked of doom and God as if warding off evil—purging it from our family. She franticly began to obsess over my health and brought me to doctors to make sure I was well.

I was fine physically, but as the strain of what began plaguing my mother mounted, I developed nervous tics and throat spasms. I felt I couldn't breathe at times and began to have terrible bowel troubles. I retreated into safe places of pretend and dolls. Colorforms, paper dolls, Barbie dolls, and books took me to another place.

I didn't want to be Karen any longer, but a super hero like Wonder Woman or Super Girl from the comic books I read who would be able to ward off the terrors, conquer the foes real or imagined.

By fourth grade my mother was hospitalized with mental issues for the first time. Since my father's parents lived next door, I stayed with them as Nonna got me ready for school. I was too frightened to ask about my mom. I wasn't sure I wanted to hear what anyone had to say. My friends never asked, and as we walked to the Catholic school we attended, I could keep up the game in my mind that a superhero girl does not cry. She is sad, but she can act normal in front of others. And so it went.

Mom's Brother, Uncle Bobby, Mom, and Her Sister, Clara

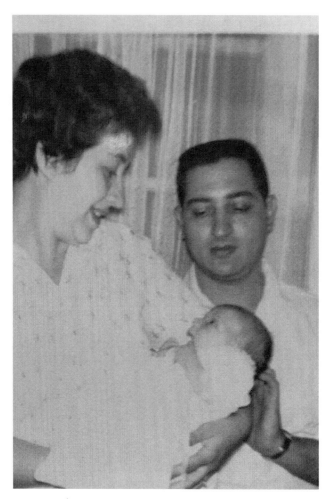

Aunt Clara and Uncle Lou With Me as a Baby

CHAPTER 5

*M*y fourth grade teacher was very sweet. Though we had many nuns in Catholic school, Miss Clark was a "regular" lady. Young, pretty and soft-spoken, she had the most soulful deep brown eyes. Her sweet demeanor helped me to have a bit of normalcy at least during the school day.

I remember she called me up to her desk after I gave her a note from home, and she asked which hospital my mother was staying in. I had no idea as I blurted out "Dixmont" that it was a state facility for the mentally ill. When Miss Clark hushed me, I felt as if I'd done something wrong. I didn't know that she was protecting me from letting other children hear what I'd said. She realized what could happen if anyone found out—how much I would be ridiculed. My family's secret was safe with her.

My teacher continued to help me as the year passed. She had a beautiful sense of how to deal with a child like me who felt lost, lonely, and scared. I was given small duties to help in the classroom: passing out papers, helping clean the blackboard. She praised my efforts at book reports and spelling bees, and I did well with my grades under her kind tutelage.

After school I walked home with my friends, saying goodbye as I entered the warm, cozy home of my Nonna and Nono. I didn't see my father until late at night. He worked at our local post office, and as soon as he was through with his work day, he would go visit my mother.

One night as he tucked me into bed, I remember him saying, "She's nutty as a fruitcake." I didn't know what fruitcake was, but unfortunately knew that nutty wasn't something good. Nuts, crazy, bonkers; everyone knew what that meant. They were words that said that a person had gone somewhere else in their mind. They were words that meant a person just might not be coming back.

In many ways, I think my father expected me to grow up a lot quicker. He had nobody else to talk with, so telling his little "Tenya," his name for me, might have offered a small bit of comfort to him. For me, it brought sadness, and I cried myself to sleep that night.

Life at my Italian grandparent's house was good though. Nonna's small kitchen constantly had a pot of something wonderful simmering on the old stove. From soups to minestrone, to delicious tomato sauce, she sang as she cooked or when she rolled out dough for homemade spaghetti. She let me help with the large wooden rolling pin or to line cookie sheets with waxed paper for the long cut strips of macaroni to dry. I helped to close raviolis with the tines of a fork. I pushed my finger into soft plump potato dough for gnocchi.

Nonna taught small Italian phrases to me of simple sentences and everyday items. She would point to the butter, *burro*, milk, *latte*, or jug of water, *bottiglia d'acqua* in her refrigerator and ask me to repeat the names back in Italian. She taught me enough to know when she wanted me to shut the light, *chiudi la luce*, or get something from the cellar, *vai a prendere il. . .* I felt proud knowing a little of her first language. Nonna was an upbeat, chubby woman who always went about singing Italian songs. She was never angry or cross. She wore her graying hair rolled up in a tight little bun. Nonna always had the scent of garlic and her favorite orchid dusting powder about her. She wore house dresses and little slip-on sandals all the time.

Nono was a quiet man who mostly enjoyed drinking wine. He sat in his cellar sometimes for hours enjoying his homemade fruit of the vine. He would come upstairs and then fall asleep in the living room in his reclining chair. Sometimes I saw him talking softly to himself and wondered about it, but then I realized he was praying.

My grandparents had a vegetable garden that took up their whole back yard. It was filled with all types of pepper plants, different sorts of tomatoes, several kinds of lettuce, garlic, onions, parsley and basil. They had a fig tree and a grape arbor built over a cozy sitting area near the back of their house; and enormous flowerbeds filled with all sorts of colorful roses, lily of the valley, geraniums, and marigolds.

Late summer had always been an especially magical time. The scents and sights of good, plowed earth, vegetables picked freshly from the vine, and the breathtaking roses became balm to me. I accompanied my grandparents into their garden for tomato picking, and the fresh green tang of the vine as it rubbed against my fingers left an indelible mark on my senses.

Later, Nonna, with a red bandana wound around her head, and an apron stained with the juices of fresh vegetables splashed all over the front, would begin braiding garlic and onions to hang from the rafters in her cool cellar. She had a gathering of Mason jars freshly boiled and ready for homemade tomato sauces, pickled peppers, mushrooms and more. Trays of parsley and basil dried in the dark; the aroma could have put a pizza shop to shame.

Watching Nonna's fingers working as she crocheted fascinated me. With my own little hook and ball of yarn, Nonna began to teach me simple stitches. I was thrilled with the lengthening chain I began and pretended to make clothes for my dolls.

Nothing was more exciting than Nonna's attic. Older homes sometimes had the extra third floor. There was a staircase hidden toward the back of my grandmother's bedroom which was like a secret entrance to the door of the walk-in attic. Two double beds were always ready for extra family. A Singer sewing machine with a foot treadle sat near an old dusty window. Cardboard boxes stuffed with yellowing newspapers held layers of voluminous old bridesmaid dresses that sparkled with glittery sequins and pretty clothing from another era. There were large steamer trunks with their slightly musty scent piled with assorted goodies—doilies, sewing boxes, hand-crocheted items and knick knacks.

An attic that was big enough to have two double beds and assorted antique furniture was better than any clubhouse. There was a small, mysterious room in one corner that had a small fire once and it still held the scent of old smoke. Yellowing, cracked linoleum lined the floor. Yet to me, it was as beautiful as a mansion.

Nonna had a tin button container I adored. My little fingers pried off the lid with a swish as I awaited the magical piles of kid's booty inside: scraps of material, old zippers, coins, and sewing thread. There were lovely rhinestone buttons, plastic buttons that looked like flowers, metal ones and opaque colored ones. It was a favorite playtime for my cousin, Anna and I, to choose favorites and pretend they were "people." Nonna's button was always the biggest one with a large sparkling stone in the center. Our mom's buttons were more conservative—plain and white. My own was light blue with a floral print and a tiny stone in the center. Buttons were just small enough to fit anywhere —to have incredible adventures, and always have a story that ended happily ever after.

Many people at that time had boarders that stayed with them—people who paid a small amount of rent for a room. Nonna's boarder was Phil, a true gentleman with a big, booming voice and great sense of humor. He worked in a local steel mill, and became like a member of the family.

My grandmother made regular Sunday dinners with homemade spaghetti or lasagna, tasty meatballs, tender veal cutlets, Italian bread, greens cooked with olive oil and garlic, and salad fresh from the garden. We drank Tom Tucker Ginger ale and Regent orange pop. Nonna always had a lovely floral tablecloth underneath, but clear plastic covered the table at all times in case we spilled something. These dinners were wonderful and even though my mother wasn't around, I felt a sense of family bonding.

Phil told silly stories which made me and my cousin, Anna, giggle during dinner. He also would get us to finish our whole plate of food by saying that whoever was the last one eating, was the "monkey." Nobody wanted this title, so I blame Phil for my weight gain and love of food later in life. Then Anna and I would help Nonna clear the table and squabble over who got to wash the dishes, and who had to dry them. Anna was older than me by several months, so somehow she always seemed to win the best of our fights.

Sometimes Nonna and Nono had friends over for card-playing nights. Wine flowed freely at the dining room table, and chatter was mostly in Italian. I sometimes sat watching them play or they tried teaching me the rules to a game of Scopa, an Italian card game. My eyes became heavy as they played late into the night, and Nonna would walk me up to her room and tuck me into her bed. She closed the door, and as I drifted to sleep, I could still hear their hearty laughter and talk.

In the morning, as the clock radio woke us, we listened to KDKA, our local station, with Jack Bogut in the morning. The soothing sound of his voice, and the way he talked about Pittsburgh always brought a sense of awe and peace to me as I lay there safe with my grandmother. She would head downstairs to turn on the old percolator coffee pot and warm the oven. Her kitchen was freezing in wintertime, and I sometimes sat and ate my bowl of cereal with an afghan draped around my body. Because Nono slept up in the attic when I was there, he sometimes woke much later than us and we wouldn't see him until afterward.

Childhood was my own Narnia world. Though there were realistically bad events, nothing could steal my imagination. Pretending became balm to me; an escapism that I sometimes wish I could still find. If I was really someone else, nothing could harm me, right? Or so I thought.

CHAPTER 6

$\mathcal{N}$othing was better than time spent with several of my favorite friends.

Patty was my first best friend. She lived only three doors away from me, so I got to know her from a fairly young age. Patty didn't like dolls, so we mostly played outdoors together. For some reason, she never knocked on my door. She walked past my house several times until I finally saw her. Her family life seemed difficult too; I saw sadness surrounding her sometimes but maybe that bonded us even more.

There was my cousin, Anna. Her family was army folks. Occasionally they would come by for long visits. They stayed in Nonna's attic. I wanted them to live near us all the time. Life seemed happier when they were around. My Aunt Lil was so much like her brother, my dad. She was funny, stable, good, and pleasant. I secretly wished she was my mother.

Anna and I were close in age and I adored her. She was the greatest and smartest girl that I knew. Her creative ideas for fun and play were magical to me. We put on small plays, sang crazy songs, and drove our grandfather to distraction by pretending to "steal" canned goods from his cellar. We also pretended to be favorite television characters,

Penny perhaps, from "Lost in Space," or Emma Peel from "The Avengers."

Diane was another, my second best friend growing up who was so much like me. We loved many of the same things. We even thought alike. She had a sweet, quiet way about her and when she stayed over, we talked late into the night about our favorite actors, singers, and movies. I always felt calmer when we were together. We played Barbie's, dressing them in magnificent outfits and made up wonderful stories for them. We became obsessed with little Hot Wheels cars—the kind that had doors that opened and closed. We made Easy Bake Oven cakes and watched tons of movies with our favorite actors.

There was Nonna's wonderful basement for plenty of mysterious happenings. An old wine cellar lay deep in a partially underground portion. It was cool and dark in there. The huge oak barrels had a constant scent of grapes that permeated the air. For little girls, it was a hiding place of villains and bad guys. Another section once was the old coal room from a time that my grandparents still had a coal furnace. Musty and forbidden, we would occasionally sneak a look into the room imagining all sorts of vile creatures.

Outside there was the grape arbor around the back of their house filled with twisted woody vines resplendent with scads of green grapes. A handmade wooden bench sat underneath, and many times that small patch of outdoors became our pretend home. There was no stopping the limit to our imaginations or the unbelievable times we kids had there.

There were also great old board games to pass the hours: *The Last Straw* where you tried not to break the plastic camel's back. There was *Mystery Date* where you either opened the door to find a dud or a handsome young man, and *Voice of the Mummy*, a particular favorite of ours. There was an actual tiny record player in that game which spoke in a creepy voice telling each player's token what to do next on the game board. Magical Colorforms, "Miss Cookie's Moon Kitchen," and paper doll sets, *Mary Poppins, Green Acres*, and "Bridal Dolls" also were all the rage at the time. How I loved anything that used imagination.

On one particular Saturday morning, Nonna had permitted me and my friend, Diane, to watch cartoons next door at my own house. I felt like a big girl. My grandmother trusted me. We were settled onto the couch with our bowls of cereal, lying around in pajamas watching *The Bugs Bunny and Road Runner Show.* My father had gone to work at the post office. I had no idea what was about to happen.

A knock on the door revealed my mother's Aunt Hilda. What could she possibly want? Nonna was next door. Why couldn't she go over to their house and bother them? This woman scared me. I always envisioned her like the wicked witch from *The Wizard of Oz.* She always seemed so morose, ready to pounce on the slightest infraction.

Before Mom was hospitalized, we used to visit her about two times a month. As a good little girl of the 1960's, I did what I was told. When Mom said we were going for a visit, I dropped whatever I was playing, and trudged the block-and-a-half with her to Aunt Hilda's darkened, creepy house.

We would sit in her living room which smelled like mothballs and something old. Her furniture was stiff and scratchy. There was no television for me. I had to listen to the two of them chatting for what felt like hours. We were hardly ever offered a glass of something to drink or one of the fresh baked goods I would sometimes smell from her little kitchen. There was never lighthearted conversation.

I wondered why my mother subjected herself to these visits. It had to be out of duty. Who would want to hear morbid, depressing discussions? I tried to feel sorry for this woman who'd had several tragedies in her life. My mom wouldn't dream of talking badly about her, though she corrected Mom a lot when we were over her house. I came to secretly dislike her.

As I let her into my house that particular Saturday, Aunt Hilda narrowed her eyes as she walked into the living room. Already I could see that she disapproved of two little girls watching cartoons. She took a short walk through the house, came back into the living room and pounced. "Why are there dishes in the sink?" she asked in what sounded like her cackling witch voice. "There's dust on the furniture, and the bathroom needs cleaned. Go make the beds. Stop watching this nonsense. You have to be grown up now and begin working around this house!"

I wanted to blubber, but I wouldn't dare cry. Not in front of my friend. With all the courage I could muster, I got up from the couch and followed the evil aunt around, taking in all my new duties. As she was leaving, Aunt Hilda said she would come back and make sure I was doing my new chores. She would be checking on me, and often.

I can remember watching my friend leave as I headed over to Nonna's house. I tried to tell my grandmother about what Aunt Hilda had said. Later that night, Dad asked me about it. Nonna had reported the whole story to him. Though I hoped he would rush right over to the witch's house and tell her off for yelling at his little girl, he did no such thing. This taught me how he would handle future crisis. My Knight-in-Shining-Armor was a peacemaker.

As I cried myself to sleep that night, vowing that I would somehow get even with that woman, a new secret terror had begun: an obsession with cleanliness. If Aunt Hilda could pop in at any old time, I'd better be ready. Everything must always be in order.

I feel tender sorrow for the little child I was. I thought I was a bad girl if beds weren't made properly, or if there was soap scum in the bathroom sink or tub. Aunt Hilda had ripped the rug from underneath the last vestiges of childhood for me. She forced me to grow up fast and had no idea about being kind to a little girl whose future was so uncertain. None of us knew the outcome for my mother. Why couldn't this awful woman show tenderness? Why couldn't she give me a hug and tell me that everything would be okay no matter what?

It was the lack of hugs at this point in my life that also stuck with me. I had no mother to smooth my hair over my brow and whisper words of love to me. I had a father who was pushed beyond measure going to work and frantically worrying over his wife and little daughter; no time for affection of any sort. And my grandparents, though wonderful, were also stoic people. I wonder how a little tender hugging would have changed me.

CHAPTER 7

The children in my fourth grade room seemed carefree and silly. I sat back watching their antics, envying them for what I felt I didn't have. I was always serious and sad, the odd one; different from others. I wished that I could be more like them. On the playground after lunch, kids slid down huge sliding boards, rode the see-saw, climbed up to the top of monkey bars enjoying themselves while I stood off to the side. Everything frightened me. I thought I would get hurt.

One day, Miss Clark told us that we were going to put on a small play for St. Patrick's Day. She worked very hard to ensure that everyone was involved and that it would be a smashing success. I had been given a lovely role which included some sort of dance. Miss Clark had told me it was a special part. I was supposed to wear a flowing-type of long skirt or dress. Since my mother was in the hospital, and my Nonna didn't understand a thing about it, I had nothing unique to wear. A girl in my class told me she would bring something for me on the day of the play. When she described it, my heart lifted. I would fit in after all. I would look pretty.

The day arrived and I was handed a very plain white, long cotton slip. It was something to be worn underneath of clothing. For some reason the girl who'd promised me a beautiful, flowing dress was unable to acquire one for me. Instead, she'd brought in a half-slip of some sort. I had no idea what to do with it. Miss Clark pulled it over my head onto what I'd worn to school that day. Humiliation crept over me, and the knowledge that I was again different from others. They all had a mom to help get them ready. I didn't know if I would ever see my mother again.

We pulled off the little play and made our teacher proud. I tried to shine. After all, Wonder Woman/Super Girl could overcome any obstacle.

At home, I still worried over Aunt Hilda's impending visits. Nothing was out of place in my house. Not one dish was unwashed. Dad was around a little more on the weekends, especially Sunday for Nonna's sit-down dinners. But the table started to feel odd, empty without my mother's presence. I wanted to cry out, "When is she coming back? *Is* she ever coming back?" But fear held me captive and my nervous tics continued. I obsessed over my throat constrictions and hyperventilation, and wondered if any other kids my age did strange, repeated gestures.

Then something unusual happened. My mother was permitted to come home for short visits at a time. She had gained a lot of weight. She had large dark circles under her eyes and a haunted look on her face. She slept so much during her time there. I felt as if she was a fragile doll that could break easily. I tried to avoid her and give her space. Nobody mentioned if she was doing well. Nobody said that life would go back to normal.

Sometimes I overheard things that the grownups said about my mom and her mental state. My grandfather muttered things like, "no good, lazy, and good-for-nothing." All I wanted was to have my family back together. I wanted my mom to smile again, and to be brave, strong, and well. If I would have known it was possible at the time, I would have prayed to God to restore her. But I didn't understand a God who would take a little girl's mommy from her. I only knew the Catholic prayers and they were not a comfort to me.

Priests and church frightened me. Confessional booths were like secret torture chambers. If I confessed that I'd missed Mass, the old priest would scold in a deep voice, "*Why* did you miss?" As if I had something to do about it at my age. They spoke of hell and punishment, and I began to confuse that with what was going on with my mother. Was this perhaps a punishment of sorts? Was my mother bad, or worse yet, was I the bad one?

I couldn't have known that my father was a praying man or others were praying too. And it would be a miracle that would eventually lead my mother back to us. But not for a long, long time.

CHAPTER 8

*C*atholic school had been all I'd known for four years. Because we belonged to a different church from the school I attended, my parents were going to have to pay much more for yearly tuition. Dad sat me down and explained that we didn't have that kind of money. I would have to go to a public school across our small town. I would have to leave the only few good friends I'd made. There was no other choice.

I'd never ridden a school bus before and it terrified me to do so. I didn't know the first thing about where to sit, or what to do. There was an odd smell on the bus that reminded me of the beer gardens we sometimes passed while riding bikes. I wondered if the driver was secretly drinking. But who was there to tell?

The public school was filled with strange, new faces—unfamiliar children. The school was huge and we changed classes. All I'd known was a one-story Catholic school. All I'd known were my best friends, Diane and Patty, and staying together in one room.

The most foreign aspect to the new school was gym class. The other kids knew what they were doing. I'd never been introduced to sports, gymnastics, or anything but kickball and dodge ball.

When we were told to tumble on rubber mats in the gym, I didn't know how to do it. When we were told to swing from uneven parallel bars, I took a zero for my grade because I'd never even heard of them before. What was a balance beam? I could barely balance myself on the pavement. I felt so out of place, so different from everyone.

Because my Nonna wouldn't understand how I felt, I chose to keep it all locked inside. I knew Dad wouldn't have time to listen to me whine, nor could he do anything about it. I secretly hated myself for not being athletic. I felt accident-prone and out of place. Even my Wonder Woman/Super Girl alias couldn't help this time.

The more popular girls made fun of me. I'd been chosen to bring some papers with one of them to the principal's office. When I walked into an empty room to lay the papers down, the popular girl turned off the light and closed the door on me as she snickered on the other side. I wouldn't cry. I was becoming emotionless because of all I had to deal with at home and now in this strange, horrible place. I started to shut down and shut out new people.

If it wasn't for one girl, Debbie, I would never have gotten through it. She became my best friend, and like two quiet outcasts, we survived together. We passed notes with little drawings. We kept to ourselves.

Our class went on a field trip once. As an innocent child, I carelessly left my purse on a chair while I threw something away in a trash can. When I returned to my seat, and it was time for lunch, I found that my money was gone. Though I emptied my little purse, nothing was to be found and I knew there had been a five dollar bill in there earlier. Again, with nobody to tell, I sat silently as unfairness wound itself around me tightening and choking.

When summer came before my sixth grade year, I rejoiced. It would be time to be with my old friends again.

Jump rope, hopscotch, hide and seek; it-tag, running, bikes, and lemonade stands. Mr. Softee ice cream truck, lightning bugs, and crickets. Scents of flowers, soft rain showers, and fresh turned earth in my grandparent's garden. Small pockets of heaven and peace on earth though short-lived.

One day, my grandmother's border, Phil, asked me and my friend Patty if we would like to go to a playground. He took us to the one at the Catholic school I'd attended.

We arrived at the playground, and Patty and I ran to climb on a set of monkey bars fashioned like a space ship. Phil sat and read the paper a bit away from us at a bench near the entrance. Three children approached us, one girl I recognized from school. Somehow Patty crept away and went over to a set of swings. I didn't see her go.

The oldest boy in the group spoke. He said something to me that was so preposterous that I had to ask him to repeat what he said once again. "I told you, touch your thing!" he barked.

"No," I answered, my stomach churning, tiny needles of fear prickled my skin. I wanted to run, but could I? What would they do if I didn't obey?

"Touch your thing!" he ordered once again.

I had no choice and hastily put a finger on the outside of my shorts. The three of them laughed like it was the funniest thing they'd ever seen. "How much does it weigh?" he asked.

Time stopped. I was trapped. My throat closed up and it was difficult to breathe. There was nothing I could do.

Just when I thought they would hurt me, Patty came running over. "Phil's ready to go," she said. Four of the best words I'd ever heard. I walked away as quickly as I could from this torturous group and I did not cry. I had no one to tell.

This behavior was completely foreign to me. I had sweetness and a very naive way about me. I was easy prey. This type of newfound fear and subsequent abuse molded my future. Mistrust became the new norm, and a fear of boys and groups of kids.

I found myself running into the house when I played outdoors if large groups of children walked down the block together. I hid until I felt safe that they were out of sight. Nervousness was normal for me; fear, a daily companion.

Just a few weeks before school began, Patty and I splashed in a small swimming pool in a yard at the side of her house. We'd persuaded her mom to let us fill it with bubbles; two little girls innocently having fun. I felt eyes upon me, and looked up to see two of the kids from the hateful playground incident looking at us.

"Aren't you the girl from the playground?" the girl I went to school with asked.

"Yes," I said. "She was there too." I pointed to Patty, trying to throw her off my scent.

"I'm gonna beat you up," the girl said to me.

Patty and I ran dripping from the pool to the safety of her back porch. We dried off and dressed quickly. We never spoke of it, our perfect day ruined.

I knew my sixth grade year would now be hell. Wasn't it enough that I had a sick mother? I had a creepy aunt that I feared, and now I would have to attend school with this terrible girl.

I began writing out a few of my feelings in a small diary I'd gotten for Christmas. Terrified that someone would find out the real me and the many fears I had, most of the writing was abbreviated and cryptically written. There was a small lock on the outside with a tiny key that fit into it. I carefully hid it away, locking the diary and parts of myself up with it. All of my worries were internalized. Though I was a very kind little girl, I sometimes thought that nobody knew the real me. I obeyed my grandparents and teachers. I was caring and respectful. Yet there were issues that stayed successfully hidden; issues that threatened to pull me into an abyss of despair.

CHAPTER 9

$\mathcal{T}$imes went from bad to worse, though I didn't know for many years afterward what almost happened—what could have happened.

One Sunday, the late summer of my sixth grade year, my mother was home with us for one of her visits. She had been back for a while. We made plans to visit my uncle, her brother who lived one town away.

We arrived around noon or so, and my cousins who were close to my age said that they were just about to go swimming at the public pool. I didn't know how to swim and didn't really want to go. My aunt and uncle said how much fun it would be, and besides, why would I want to sit around listening to a bunch of adults talking.

I borrowed a swimsuit from the cousin who was closest to my age. I didn't enjoy my time at the pool. If a group of teenagers came near, I would climb out, terrified that they were going to dunk me. I spend the whole day jumping in and out of the pool because I was scared of water and terrified of any groups of young, wild boys. It was a horrible day to be followed by something worse.

My uncle came by to pick us up a little later. When we arrived back at their house, my parents were nowhere to be seen. It had finally happened. I'd been totally abandoned. My aunt and uncle said that I would be spending the week with them. Something happened to my mother, and she might be away for a while.

My throat closed. I couldn't catch a breath. Though my father called me and calmly tried to explain that it was best for me to be with this family for a short time, all I wanted was to be with him. There was nothing I could do about it. I had no idea what was going on. No idea that something really bad, maybe worse than anything we'd already gone through was happening.

I wore my cousin's clothes for a week, attended school a few days with her as a guest, since her classes had already begun, and hung around with her friends who were way too wild for me. I felt out of place. There was nothing for me but fear and sadness. It felt like the longest week of my life.

It wasn't that my aunt and uncle were unkind, but I wished they wouldn't have been so secretive about my mother. I sometimes wished one adult would try to explain her behavior to me.

When my father called again, I begged him to please come pick me up. He said that he would, and he told me that mom was stable, which meant that she was going to be okay. When my mother returned from this hospital visit, she had bandages wrapped around her wrists. I didn't know why. I never asked, and nothing was spoken about it at the time.

As I suspected, sixth grade began with a bang for me. The girl who had promised violence was everywhere. Anytime she saw me, she threatened, "I'm gonna beat you up." I was meek and mild; a peace lover. I'd never been in a fight. Though I got ready for school each day with a heavy heart, I never told my father or grandparents. Everyone already had way too much to deal with.

I still lived with the pretending game in my head. I pictured myself as someone else—anyone to escape the nightmare. I pretended to be a famous singer or actor, but no longer Wonder Woman. I was not this shy, scared little girl. I was someone special.

And then a small miracle occurred. Another schoolgirl named Judy, someone I didn't know that well, stood up for me. She was tough, outspoken, a fighter. When the girl threatened me in front of Judy, my hero told her that I was okay, and to leave me alone. I was never bothered again. And a few months proceeded with a bit more normalcy.

I often wondered about Judy through the years. How she must have had a sense of understanding about her for someone as frightened as me. There were many things I never questioned, however, and this was one of them. I accepted this gift and breathed a little easier.

CHAPTER 10

*D*uring one of my mother's longest hospital visits, Dad warned me about any phone calls that might come from her. I wondered why. Didn't Dad know how much I wanted to talk to my mother, and how much I missed her?

In pure Dad fashion, he bluntly said to me: "Your mother is not doing well right now. In fact, she sometimes doesn't know who she is."

My young brain could not process that. I was a kid, for goodness sakes. Why had Dad told me that? I didn't understand.

He added, "Mom might call and ask you a question. I want you to be prepared."

Question?

"If Mom asks you who you *are*, make sure you ask her who she *is* first."

Enough already. Wait a minute. Why can't I just tell her who I am? *I'm Karen, your daughter, Mom. And I miss you so much.*

But Dad went on. "She thinks everyone is somebody religious now. So if she asks if you're the Virgin Mary, don't answer right away. She might think she's Mary, and well, you both can't be the same person."

Throat spasm . . . hyperventilation. Now my mother doesn't know us. She thinks she is the Blessed Mother. It was all too much. To picture my mother in the throes of total insanity became an obsession for me. I wondered about her at all hours of the day and night. How could it be that she didn't know me, her daughter and only child? I wouldn't accept this. I couldn't.

Luckily, Mom never called me during the worst of this bout of madness. If she'd asked, I may have had to tell her that I was Scout Finch from *To Kill a Mockingbird*. Scout wasn't afraid of anything.

When her instability cleared a bit, they allowed my mother to return home again for short visits. I was afraid of affection, afraid to get close to her. After all, she could leave again quickly without a moment's notice and I would again be motherless.

Mom saw devils everywhere around her. I became so worried that I pictured Satan living in our basement or fireplace. I had terrifying dreams at night and woke up so frightened that I lost my voice when I tried to scream.

One weekend, my step-grandma invited us over for dinner. Grand-pap, Mom's father, came to pick us up in his car. I didn't care for him. He often smelled of whiskey and beer, and when he visited us, he'd tease me. One time my friend Diane and I had built a huge fort out of several decks of playing cards on my kitchen table. Mom was proud of us and said she couldn't wait to show it to my dad when he got home from work that night.

Grandpap stopped over that particular day, drunk and weaving when he walked in. He proceeded to plop into a seat at the kitchen table whereupon our whole card house fell to pieces. He never even noticed. I left the room and cried.

He made fun of me calling me a baby at other times when he visited. I saw how my mother reacted to him. I sensed an over-whelming fear. I, too, grew to fear and dislike him.

The day he came to pick us up for dinner, a friend was playing over my house at the time, and I asked if she could come with us. Mom still had that look on her face, a mistrusting, constantly scared look. Her weight had blossomed upward of almost three hundred pounds, and black circles still rimmed her eyes.

My step-grandma, Mary, greeted us and sat us all down for dinner. Afterward, my friend and I went out to play in the back yard.

So far, the day had been uneventful. It was nice seeing Grandma Mary. She was a big, good woman with a nurturing nature. My mother's father had married her after his wife had died young.

But to Mom, Grandpap became the real devil. She pictured him as red, with horns. He was evil and was going to hurt her. She must have panicked because my step-Grandma came outside with her as Mom acted like a total weirdo to me.

I was appalled. She was behaving erratically in front of my friend. Nobody would want to be around me pretty soon. My mother began saying scary things about her father. She said he was Satan. She said he would hurt all of us.

Grandma Mary, in a loud booming voice, pretended to "cast Satan" out of Grandpap and into the little Chihuahua dog in the next yard. It seemed to calm my mother down, but I wasn't calm. I didn't think our lives would ever change, and would only grow worse. This type of behavior was unusual and very hurtful to me. Soon everyone would know that I had a weird mother. And perhaps someday, I, too, would behave this way. Perhaps it was inherited.

I wanted her to go away again. I didn't know this odd changeling of a mother. But I made up my mind right then: I would *never* be like her.

This was the time that my father and I grew closer. He went out of his way to see that I was happy.

We watched football games together while Dad carefully explained the rules of the game to me. I saw that football was something that made my father happy. He whistled and cheered when his team scored. I sat back laughing at his antics.

My father also made up his own silly language. Everyday items took on a new meaning with Dad's zany words. I think it was a way to escape our serious problems and I loved him all the more for it. Cousins, friends, and pets were called different names. By then everyone thought my father was the greatest. He became known as the uncle who made everyone laugh, and the secret saint for putting up with all he did.

My father kept beautiful roses around our house. I learned how to care for them and followed him around as he took the time to share special tips with me. I worked side by side with him taking care of our yard.

When my father brought home a crystal radio kit that we would build together as a little project, it cemented my admiration for him. He also brought a wood-burning set, a rock tumbler, several paint-by-number kits—anything we could do together. When he brought an NFL football game home with the little men that vibrated all over the playing field, I thought it was the neatest thing I'd ever seen.

We took time painting our prospective "teams" with colors of our choosing. The little plastic men were so tiny that we painted them with toothpicks dipped into small bottles of craft paint. Of course Dad picked Pittsburgh Steeler's black and gold colors, while I chose blue and silver. Then we'd watch our little guys run down the field with the tiny foam football held in their miniscule hands. I never quite understood the rules of this game, but I loved it and I had my daddy all to myself.

Perhaps life would be okay with just one parent especially when that parent was as good as my father. How he had time to spend with me after working all day and then with everything he did for Mom, was quite beyond my scope of reason. All I knew, affection had taken the form of fun craft projects that took me out of the crisis of the moment and transported me to a safer place.

CHAPTER 11

*W*inters were magical when I was a child. I adored snow and bundled up any chance I could to go outside and play. Whether we kids made a snowman, snow fort, or had the occasional snow battle, nothing seemed better, cleaner, or more amazing.

Snow-covered bushes whispered in the winter winds. Snowflakes sparkled like gems strewn on the hedges and grass. We stuck our tongues out to catch them falling and thought it tasted like spun sugar. We tied ropes to our sleds and pulled each other along.

We awoke Sunday, Valentine's Day, 1971 to a huge snowfall. My father went outside to shovel the sidewalks at my grandparent's house and then ours. Mom had been home again for a short time.

I sat in Dad's recliner near our big front picture window watching the flakes that still floated lazily in the air. I had a bowl of crunchy apple cereal perched on my lap while our dog, Buffy, slept nearby. The children's show *Davey and Goliath* played on television. Though my father and I sometimes went to church, today we decided to stay home to keep watch over Mom. Her mental state was still precarious, but there had been small patches of light in the darkness.

I listened to the scrape of the shovel as it dug into the deep piles of snow and hit the cement sidewalk underneath. I'd asked Dad if he needed help, but he said he didn't. Looking out the window at all the glistening snow, I couldn't wait to go outside and play.

Mom was upstairs in the bathroom when another sound thudded right above me. We had a big, old-fashioned Bible that Mom kept on the edge of the bathtub. It had fallen off the tub before and made a big thump. I thought that's what happened. I paid no mind to it.

Buffy awoke with a start. She ran to the bottom of the steps and began growling. I tried calling her back, wondering what on earth she was making all the fuss about.

"Buffy, come here," I said as I put my cereal bowl down and headed over to her. That is when I heard the awful sound coming from above. It was a loud gurgling snore; a sound like nothing I'd ever heard before. Should I go up and see what it was? Did Mom go back to bed and fall asleep only to begin snoring?

Something didn't feel right. I'm glad I chose the correct course of action. I ran to our front door and called out to my father. "Dad, come here! Something's wrong with Mom!"

I would never know how those words affected my poor father. Just when life would settle into a bit of normalcy, something new and foreign would come along and throw a wrench into our daily lives. My father dropped his shovel and sprinted into the house. He told me to stay in the living room and ran up the steps two at a time.

Moments later, he called down to me, "Kar, call Phil next door. Tell him to call an ambulance. Something's wrong with Mom."

I dialed the rotary phone with fingers shaking. It was happening again. Our world was crumbling with something new—something that sounded like growling.

It would be many years later that I found out what happened that day. Mom told me that she had awakened feeling extremely shaky and weak. As she sat on the toilet, a feeling overcame her and she keeled over right into the bathtub. The sound I'd heard was the sounds of a death rattle—something no little child should have to hear. When Dad first ran up the stairs, he found her face-down in the tub, and began rubbing her back. She was only slightly conscious.

The paramedics arrived and had to bring my mother down on a sling-type of gurney because she was so heavy. I sat at the phone bench at the bottom of the steps watching while Mom called out to me, "Don't worry about anything, Kar. Just have fun."

Dad followed the ambulance to a hospital, while I waited at Nonna's house for word of my mother's condition. Her parting words to me had sounded so final, like I was never going to see my mother again. Each time there was a little bit of normalcy something came along and brought instability to my world again.

None of us knew what had happened at the time, but we later found out that my mother had a cardiac arrest. She had begun dieting because of her blossoming weight. A local doctor had given her water pills, and her potassium level fell dangerously low due to the rapid water weight loss.

When Dad felt that my mother was stable and in good hands, he started to leave the hospital later in the afternoon. As he walked down the hallway, he heard: Code Blue! He knew it was for Mom.

Though my mother miraculously survived the cardiac arrest, she said to my father later that night, "Rich, I'm not afraid of dying." It wouldn't be until my teenage years that I found out the reason.

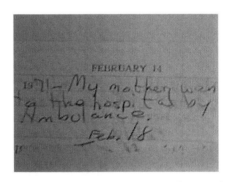

Actual Diary Entry When Mom Went to the Hospital

CHAPTER 12

I can't look back and say that every memory I carry was one of sadness. Growing up in a small town was magical at times. Small steel towns have their secrets. Children know how to have adventures around those secrets.

There were neighbors to fear, cranky old spinsters who knew everyone's business; moody fathers of friends that you had to tiptoe around; drunks that stumbled home after a stint at the local beer garden, smelling of stale cigarettes and booze. When we kids rode our bikes in the neighborhood, we imagined all sorts of mysteries behind closed doors.

There was a special-needs man who was a large part of my childhood. His name was Terry and he spoke of nothing but tragedies. He was probably in his late teens when we children got to know him. I would see his fire-engine red head appear as he took a walk around the block. "Run," we would all say. "Hide."

But my mother saw something different in him. Though Terry spoke of awful events from all over town, and it scared my mother greatly, she was able to see beyond her fear. She saw into his innocent heart and realized that nobody wanted to spend time with him.

When she was home over the course of those summers, my mother taught me a great lesson. She taught me kindness. She helped me to realize how lonely Terry was; that he didn't have a friend in the world. His talk of the happenings in our town were the only excitement in his life—a way to possibly sound heroic as he spoke of these events.

I felt sorry for him after that and I always gave him time to speak. I practiced listening and then after a bit, would politely excuse myself saying that I had to go home.

There were also sweet people like my next door neighbors who had a creaky porch swing that they would allow me to sit on every so often. And sometimes as the husband watered his flowers with a hose, he would squirt us children as we walked past and look away, feigning innocence as we giggled uncontrollably.

There were little outdoor parties that my friend Patty and I would gather small feasts of junk food: mini donuts, crackers, cookies, and cakes. Sometimes we would hang a huge blanket over the railing of her back porch and eat in the cozy tent we'd created.

We pretended our bikes were cars as we rode along the sidewalks. We would stop at the red lights and go on green. We played countless hide-and-seek games, board games, and swam in little inflatable pools in the summer. We tried to make outdoor carnivals, and pretended to sail away in grape crates to what my grandparents affectionately called The Old Country.

Our family always had a pet cat or dog, something my mother adored. Animals and nature were a comfort to her. If I could only see beyond her sickness to the woman inside who was crying to get out, crying to make herself known for who she really could be. Oh how I wanted to love her.

During the ins and outs of my mother's battle with mental illness, she found a therapist who was able to get through to her. Vinnie, as he was known, became her "Bridge over Troubled Waters" and began to lead my mom out of the darkness. A doctor and a nurse had also worked well with Mom in her recent hospital stay, along with my mother's best friend, Helen.

There were meetings held for those who were going through various nervous issues. After my mother came home from the hospital, she and Helen began to talk on the phone. To me, Helen was my mother's savior at the time; a good friend with an upbeat attitude and powerful words of healing.

There was never a true diagnosis, but just like that, one day my mother arrived home from one of her particularly lengthy hospital stays never to leave us again.

I noticed a dramatic change. The dark circles were gone from under her eyes, and her face glowed. When she talked, she spoke clearly, and made complete sense. Confusion, anxiety and sadness had vanished, and I saw lightness in her step that I'd never seen before. I was so elated to have a normal family once again that I never asked about the transformation.

Only Dad seemed to know something the rest of us didn't. A huge burden had been lifted from his shoulders, and like a secret he meant to keep, Dad didn't talk openly about the fact that a miracle had occurred. In the quiet of his heart, he knew.

Laughter replaced hushed voices and secrecy. Warm conversation and affection rooted my parents' love more deeply. Life settled into the kind of boring routine I'd envied from my friends.

My parents decided that it was time to make a clean start in our lives. We were going to move to a much quieter, wooded area. I'd grown up on a main thoroughfare in town and we were used to traffic at all hours of the day and night. We were even used to car accidents, and occasionally our beloved pets being killed on the road. The new house seemed like a dream. We would be moving away from my grandparents and my best friends, but a fresh new life was what we all needed. The new place was only ten minutes away in the same town, but it felt like another state.

I'd gotten to the point that I even believed our house was cursed. Maybe it was all that we'd gone through with Mom, but it was with a light heart that I closed the door on that chapter of my life.

CHAPTER 13

The day they brought me to the new house on Highland Avenue, I saw that it would be a place of true happiness. First of all there were two back yards! A smaller one bordering the woods with a rustic fire pit and the main yard with trees and so much greenery. I'd grown up in the cement jungle with barely a patch of grass.

The new ranch-style home had the most adorable screened porch out back—perfect for viewing nature and the little raccoons that would soon become like friends in a Disney movie. There was a wood-paneled basement with custom-made wooden bar, and even though my parents weren't drinkers, it was the perfect place for a pre-teenage girl to listen to music with friends. It seemed that Diane and I even grew closer when I moved. She stayed with us so much that people mistook us for sisters sometimes.

Dad put up a ping pong table. He and Mom played competitively against one another and then I tried to learn too. Because Dad had played during his time overseas when he was in the Korean War, he knew trick shots and how to spike the ball. Mom pretended to be mad at him, but then they ended up laughing like children.

My room had two twin beds and large windows that viewed the

glorious back yard. My parents' room was huge and also situated right next door to mine. No more nighttime fears. No wondering if my mom was gone. I felt safe and secure.

The house was situated on a quiet road with hardly any traffic. I rode my bike right in the middle of the street. On a summer night, we heard the chirping of crickets, and during the day, the sweet music of birds. I'd grown up on a main thoroughfare and had heard nothing but the sound of cars and trucks day and night.

I fell in love with this home immediately. Our family spent many happy hours seated at a small picnic table on the screened porch. From there we could watch the new wildlife that was so foreign to us. Beside raccoons there were also squirrels, rabbits, deer, and so many different types of birds. I'd never seen all of these creatures up close before.

Mom talked with the raccoons and then began to hand feed them. It got to the point that she gave them names. They weren't afraid of her at all. My father always called her St. Francis because of the way all animals flocked to her. Every living creature seemed to adore her.

Mom and Dad listened to classical music records and opera. They bought albums with Disney movie music and played it loudly through the house. Dad always pretended to conduct an orchestra that only he could see. Mom thought she could hit the high opera notes, but I thought it sounded like nails on a chalkboard when she sang. Life took on an exquisite difference when music filled the house. Dad loved waltzes and Beethoven, Mom adored Andrew Lloyd Weber and Tchaikovsky.

On lazy, hot, humid summer days, our family dressed in long-sleeved clothing and pants for our annual trek into the woods of Old Economy Park. Mom said, "You don't want mosquito bites all over you," or, "Those blackberry bushes have thorns." We never questioned her and off we drove in a car without air-conditioning with the windows wide open and scents of summer flying by.

It was early in the day when we reached the park. The long dry, un-cut grass near the trails that were blazed into the woods tried to tickle my clothing as I waded into it. The cicadas sang their unceasing song in the trees above, rasping out sounds only they could understand. Not a breath of air stirred, but the birds called out warnings to one another that their perfect world was soon to be invaded.

Dad always gave me a long stick as we began our walk into the woods. "For snakes," he said, though thankfully I never saw one. We did find hoards of delectable blackberries bursting ripe and juicy, and although a few made it into my mouth during picking, most of them plunked into the buckets we carried with the promise of pies and jellies.

When we came out of the woods hours later, Dad challenged Mom to a game of "hit the apple on the center of the tree." Several gnarly trees were lined up, their wild green fruits rotting at their base, worm-holed and oozing. My parents counted how many times each of them would hit the tree with the small projectile, and it became a contest every time. I never chose sides but cheered each of them on enjoying their silly taunting and name-calling.

After a snack of cheese and crackers and Lemon Blend from a thermos, we packed Dad's trunk with pails and bushels, bringing home a few of nature's tiniest bug creatures with us as they clung for dear life to the stems of our prizes.

We waved goodbye to another late summer, another trek into deep woods, and I felt perfectly safe, innocent, and very much alive.

Where Narnia ended in the best of my childhood, it began in an even more beautiful new way. I was almost a teenager and everything stood fresh before me.

CHAPTER 14

*S*omething was wrong in my seventh grade year. I stood
before the full length mirror in my new bedroom and tried to
stand straighter. As I was dressing one day, I'd noticed it. One side of
my body had the shape that a young teen girl's body should have,
where the hips flare slightly larger than the waist. The other, my right
side seemed oddly misshapen. I tried to think that it might be normal
—a way of my body changing as hormones progressed. I put it out of
my mind as school began.

School was within walking distance that year. It was located only a
block away from where I lived, and I began to meet all sorts of great
new friends, one of whom I keep to this day, Goldie.

Goldie was funny and sweet. We laughed together constantly. We
made cassette tapes with hilarious radio shows and sang goofy songs.
We were able to talk about boys—something that was new and
wonderful. I was in love with everyone. My mother used to tell me I
was in love with love itself.

One day in my seventh grade year, a boy started to call me names
and made fun of me. When I told my mother later in the day, she said
that all boys do that when they start to like a girl. It was their way of

talking to girls since they are so immature. I believed her for a little while.

Then it got to the point that other boys in the group would taunt me, making fun of the way I walked, and how my pants looked on me. I had all but forgotten about viewing myself in the mirror with my slightly crooked shape. But these boys noticed it, and they were relentless.

Once again in my life, school became a burden. Every day was torturous. The name-calling and imitation of my walk hurt so badly that I wanted to stay home. One day it was particularly bad, and I just left the school without telling anyone. I got in a bit of trouble for this, but couldn't explain why I did it.

Why was this happening now when my family life was so much better? My mother was becoming a friend to me. It was at a point that we were able to talk about anything. In my eyes, she was the smartest person I knew. Yet, it seemed she couldn't help me with this. I felt once again alone.

I sat on my mother's bed one Saturday while we chatted. The scents from our kitchen were heavenly—some sort of cinnamon rolls or pecan loaves. Mom's baking had become legendary. Everything seemed to turn out perfectly from what I'd thought of as her magical kitchen.

Mom began to rub and scratch my back as we talked. It hadn't been easy at first letting her touch me. From all the barriers I'd put up in my early childhood, it had been more difficult to pull those walls down. But her touch felt good, and then she suddenly stopped.

"Kar," she said, using her nickname for me. "What's this?" Her hand rested on part of my back near my right shoulder blade.

I jumped up from the bed, and screamed, "It's nothing!" But I knew better. There was something very wrong with me, and my mother had discovered it.

She spoke with Dad later that day, and they decided to make an appointment with an orthopedic specialist in Pittsburgh.

As we drove the half hour or so into town, I asked my mom many questions. "Do you think I'll need surgery?"

"No," she said. "I would imagine they have other ways to straighten your back."

"You're not going to let them do surgery, though, if they insist?" I asked.

"Honey, let's not worry about that. You're going to be fine."

After several poses for x-rays in the orthopedic office, the stern-looking doctor sat down with me and my parents.

"Your daughter has scoliosis—curvature of the spine," he said matter-of-factly. "The only way to help her is through major surgery."

My eyes welled over and spilled with tears. Mom joined in with me as dad sat stoically.

"She'll have to go to Children's Hospital. She'll have surgery to correct the curve, and a full plaster body cast. She will be in the hospital three weeks. Any questions?"

Nope. No questions from two sniveling ladies, and certainly none from my father. My parents accepted the doctor's diagnosis and took a book home from the office that diagrammed all sorts of horrors. I would need a spinal fusion, and it would not be an easy surgery.

Part of me was a bit smug. I thought of those awful boys making fun of me half of the school year. Yeah, what would they do now when they realized they were making fun of someone who was really crippled? They'd be sorry.

In June of 1972, my parents and I arrived at Children's Hospital of Pittsburgh. It loomed before me like an architectural nightmare—one where I would soon be staying.

When I was ushered to the orthopedic floor, I saw children in all sorts of horrible contraptions. There were kids with metal circles called halos piercing their heads; kids with gigantic plaster casts encasing their bodies. The smell of fear and antiseptic permeated the air, and I was going to have to breathe it for three full weeks.

The tests were painful and humiliating. They shot excruciating dye into my spine for more pictures, and they snapped poses of me without any clothes. When the day came for the first full body cast, I thought I would faint from fear.

Luckily, I'd made some wonderful friends in my hospital ward. One girl in particular, Martha, was the mother hen over all of us girls.

A little older than most, she had already gone through what I was about to have done. And she kept her explanations light and positive.

Me, the girl who was afraid of her own shadow was now going to have to face things that would make most grown-ups cringe.

The nurses arrived early one morning, injected a relaxing drug into my upper thigh to help make me drowsy and they wheeled me away from my parents to place the first plaster cast around my body.

I was placed onto a sling-type contraption, suspended in the air, as the staff worked quickly winding the plaster soaked gauze around and around me. When I was finished, I looked like a turtle. There was a plaster head rest behind my head. The cast began at my shoulders and the bulk of it reached all the way down to my hips. The sides would be cut and the back part removed before the surgery.

My parents were my strength in this difficult time. It's funny because I never thought about Mom's earlier years and her mental problems. She spoke to the doctors and nurses with authority. She talked lovingly and reassured me at all times.

Mom brought me all sorts of cards from friends and family members filled with cheerful greetings and well-wishes. She even brought a good friend I'd made in the new school, Carol, to visit me. My mother talked with other parents and their children in the ward, and became a spokesperson for all who had any questions.

Dad handled it all differently. He used humor as his balm. He made fun of the doctors and nurses, giving them secret names and identities behind their backs, all meant to make me laugh. He drew silly pictures on paper for me.

On one particular day, my parents hadn't been able to visit due to severe flooding and road closures. I lay in my hospital bed unable to move, crying by myself. I heard a little commotion and excited voices. Somebody special was coming to visit us that day. I grew curious.

Fred Rogers, the Pittsburgh legend and icon, the kindly public television persona was our special visitor. I'd loved his show and watched him all the time. His sweet manner and the way he'd introduced pretending as normal and good, were things I had naturally embraced.

As Mr. Rogers came up to my hospital bed, he reached out a hand and gently touched my arm. "What a pretty girl," he said. His words were tender and the look on his face, so compassionate. There was something about him that always seemed to know what to say to every person. He was a beautiful soul and this was a once in a lifetime dream come true for me. The fact that I'd been feeling ugly, different, and misshapen, and Fred Rogers had said those particular words to me gave me a kind of hope I'd not expected.

~

One of the scariest risk factors for surgery was paralysis. It was too much to think about. I needed the surgery but it could leave me unable to walk ever again. I cried into my pillow every night in that hospital ward.

My parents assured me that I would come through this surgery. If they had concerns, they never shared them in front of me. With strength and grace, they stayed by my side exuding confidence.

I remember a few moments before I was put onto the operating table that I began sobbing. I didn't want to go through with it. Surgery lasted around ten hours or so, and thankfully when they woke me up and asked me to move my legs I was able to do so.

I drifted in and out of consciousness in a private room. There was a tube that snaked from my nose into my stomach because I wasn't able to eat. For some reason, I hated that most of all. Other tubes, intravenous solutions were placed into veins in my arms and hands. I saw all sorts of psychedelic colors as the morphine worked its magic.

Days later, I was transferred back into the ward with other girls. I was now the sage, the one to help others who were about to go through their own trying times. I had to learn to walk again by first pushing a chair in front of myself, and then learned to balance the new body cast that was fabricated for me before I left Children's Hospital for good.

Dad's Brother, my Uncle Joe, Dog, Buffy, and Me in My Body Cast

Mom's Father, My Grandpap, Nonna, Nono, Dad, Me in Body Cast,
Grandma Mary, Uncle Joe, Aunt Catherina

CHAPTER 15

$\mathcal{T}$he summer of my convalescing period after Children's Hospital cemented my relationship with Mom. I was in a new body cast and couldn't move around very well. My mother did everything she could to make me smile. She arranged the bed in my room so that I could see directly into the kitchen where she pretended to be the magic chef, explaining all sorts of recipes to me as she cooked and baked. She bought me countless books and drawing paper. Mostly, we had our first serious conversations about life.

I had never known some of the things my mother had gone through—things that may have contributed to her earlier problems. She felt that I was old enough to hear them.

Mom told me stories about growing up with an abusive, alcoholic father. She told me that she'd been unwanted as a baby, and her mother had almost aborted her. She said that the one person who showed her unconditional love had been her older sister who had passed away when I was eight years old. No wonder that year had been hard for all of us. I could see the patterns of her life now. It became clear that she'd never been weak. My mother had only wanted to be loved.

It was during this time that my mother told me that she'd had a secret name for me. She called me her "shining star." Like a blazing trail of light, I was always the one thing Mom could come back to. When she knew nothing else, she still knew me. She said I'd been like a beacon of hope to guide her home. It was a title that rooted my love deeply for my mom. I knew from that moment forward that nothing could take her away from us again and she would only grow stronger. She certainly felt that it was time for me to hear the whole story.

In 1968, around the time my mother's sister Clara became deathly ill, Mom told me that she began getting incapacitating panic attacks. No longer able to go out of the house, or have the energy to get through each day, she retreated into a safe place within herself; a place where nobody could hurt her.

Mom said that in the worst of it, the time we had visited my Uncle Bobby's house, she had felt so low that she knew the world would be better off without her. She'd thought that God was displeased with her, and that she'd failed everyone who cared about her. She admitted to me that she had gone into the bathroom at her brother's house and looked for razor blades. She cut into her wrists hoping to end her life. She'd felt as if she was purging the bad from her, and nothing, even the thought of me at that time could keep her from the worst of the darkness.

Dad must have known she was gone a little too long, and when he checked on her, had found her in the bathroom, though not unconscious. She'd been taken to another mental facility at the time and even was given electro-shock therapy.

Sitting at the kitchen table as my mom unloaded her guilt, I hurt very deeply for her. The fact that she wanted to die to get away from the pain she was feeling became evident to me. Yet I wondered: *Didn't she love me? Did she really want to leave me and my dad?* A small flame of anger stirred within me. I needed time to process what she told me.

But as more of her story unfolded, I began to understand the lost girl she'd been. It was as if the scales fell from my own eyes. Though it completely shocked me, I wondered: *How could I be angry about this? How could I judge her?*

Even though she attempted suicide, my mother knew now just how fortunate she'd been that she had not succeeded. Sitting across the table from me in my huge plaster body cast, Mom said God must have known how much I would need her.

My mother was able to make light of the other times—times she hadn't known who she was in her religious mania. We giggled about that together, able to find a little humor in what had been gut-wrenching sadness.

Mom told me about the doctor, nurse, and therapist who had brought her out of the darkness. I listened in awe as she told me about the mental hospital. I pictured archaic rooms and crabby old nurses. My mother, even in the throes of her own problems, quickly had become caregiver for many of the other ladies on her ward. One woman who wouldn't eat for anyone else let Mom feed her. She listened to others compassionately even though she felt she would never recover. She gave herself willingly to those she thought were much worse than she was.

If my mother was asking for forgiveness, I didn't feel I was the one to give it. For me there was nothing to forgive. I saw it all completely before me; her childhood and fears. And even though she'd had a wonderful man, my dad, it hadn't been enough to keep her from losing sight of who she was.

Dad's love, she said, had certainly helped her. Mom brought me into her bedroom and opened a drawer in her nightstand. It was filled with beautiful cards and letters from my father to her through the years. The love that was poured into the sometimes hastily written notes came from deep in Dad's heart and soul. He had never thought of abandoning her. He had loved her through the worst of it. I sat looking through some of the most intimate and loving words.

When we finished talking about her illness, Mom looked at me. "Do you think any differently about me now?" she asked.

"No, never," I answered. "I see nothing but courage. I am completely in awe of you."

"I have one more thing to tell you," Mom said as we walked back into the kitchen. "It's the most amazing part of all this."

She made herself a cup of coffee while I popped open a can of ginger ale. I settled back to listen.

"You remember when I had the cardiac arrest, Kar?" she asked.

"Uh, yeah, of course," I said. How could I forget that day? We'd almost lost her.

"Well, you see when they took me to the hospital and got me stable, something else happened. When Dad went to leave, I got worse. That's when I had the arrest."

Mom's eyes lit up. A look of peace and beauty crossed her features. Her hands rested on the table clasped together as she continued.

"I remember being 'there' one minute, and then gone the next. I saw a long darkness in front of me, kind-of like a tunnel."

I held my breath waiting for what she might say next. Her face was serene and her demeanor, calm. She'd been waiting to tell me this for a long time.

"I felt like I was moving down the tunnel, I guess. And the further I traveled; a feeling wrapped me in complete love, warmth, radiance—as if I was the only person in the world that mattered." She paused before adding, "It's almost indescribable, and I wish I could explain it better, but I know I was almost in God's presence."

"What?" I asked.

"Yes. But then I felt myself being pulled back, like the way I'd gone into the tunnel. I heard the doctor say, 'She's back!' and then I opened my eyes."

It seemed the doctor and nurses had to use the defibrillator paddles on my mother as she had the cardiac arrest. They knew they were losing her and only had moments to save her.

"Kar," Mom looked directly at me. "I'm not afraid to die. If that's where we're all headed, it was the most incredible love I've ever felt."

I knew a little of what Mom was talking about. I'd heard stories like this before. Although this was the 1970's when it wasn't fashionable talking of such things, I knew my mother had gone through something magnificent; something with God written all over it. Though I'd almost lost her twice, she was here for a reason. That reason would present itself in many ways in the years to come.

CHAPTER 16

"$\mathcal{I}$ think I have the flu," Mom said one day.

She'd been vomiting for a while especially in the mornings when she first awoke.

I'd been free from my body cast for a few months. My body looked normal and my outlook on life, so much better than it had been in a long time.

"Yeah, I wonder," I said to her. The clothes basket sat next to both of us on her bed as we sorted socks and folded towels and washcloths.

"It's been going on a little too long," Mom said. "I think I'll make a doctor's appointment this week."

My parents returned from the doctor visit preoccupied and a bit suspicious in their actions.

"What did the doctor say?" I asked.

"Oh, nothing much," Mom replied. "He says I need to rest."

What I hadn't known was this:

"Mrs. Mattia, I've got some news for you. Blood work shows you're pregnant."

"What?" Mom asked a bit incredulous, a bit confused. "I'm a little old, aren't I, doctor?"

"I assure you that you are not too old. But I have to be frank with you. Considering your past miscarriages and the hemorrhaging, it could be devastating to your health. I want you to consider an abortion."

There, it was out. A horrible word, a frightening time. Mom didn't hesitate however in her response. "Doctor," she said, "This baby is a gift from God. For all I've been through and all my losses, I am going to have this baby or die trying." She never wavered in her decision. But since the doctor had scared her with his advice, she and Dad knew this could be a difficult pregnancy and delivery.

When I learned that my mother was going to have a baby, I couldn't stop smiling. I didn't know about the worry, or what had been said. I only knew I wasn't going to be alone any longer. I would have a baby brother or sister! I would be the best big sister possible.

Eight months later, my mom went into labor, and I sat at my grandparent's house once again as I had done as a child. This time, I was almost fourteen, however. I prayed like never before and believed with my whole heart that everything was going to be wonderful.

When we received the call later after we went to sleep, my Nonna came into the room and with her cute Italian accent said, "Your mama have a baby boy. Everybody doin a good."

Suddenly I couldn't sleep. I wanted the whole world to know about my new brother! I wanted to throw a party in his honor and wished I could visit my mother right then. I had to content myself with visiting the hospital with Dad the next day. And from the minute I saw that beautiful baby, I fell completely in love with him.

They named my brother Matthew Richard, but for some reason, his middle name stuck and we ended up calling him Ricky. He was a chunky, adorable baby, and like a second mother, I did everything I could for him and to help my mom.

I doted on him like a mother hen. I watched him when my parents needed a little time together. Having a little brother was the best thing that could have happened to me. No longer a lonely, only child, I felt there was another part of our family to share the love.

As Ricky grew through the years, he was an answer to prayer. We had so much fun and so many laughs together. Though I was so much older, it never mattered. We got along well and there were times we were more like friends than siblings. We bonded over "Star Wars" and MTV music videos. We commiserated over unfair situations and different people. Life certainly got more interesting and changed for the better with the addition of my brother.

Mom and Dad weren't big travelers. They did find one special place, however, that they vacationed with me and my brother. It was a quaint, old amusement park called Conneaut Park, only an hour-and-a-half away.

We packed the car and then Dad drove while my brother and I chatted about all of the fun things we would do once we got there. As always, the last turn on the winding country road showed the top of the old, wooden roller coaster peeking out from the trees. It gave my stomach a jolt of excitement. I'll never forget how the sight of that coaster, the sound of it whooshing and whomping along the track, and the laughter and thrill screams from countless people who rode it, alerted me to the fact that our family had just arrived at Conneaut Lake Park. And just as it had many times before, the coaster didn't fail to disappoint.

One of our favorites was a scary dark ride called "The Devil's Den." After unpacking our things at the grand and allegedly haunted Hotel Conneaut, we would run over to the "Den" and await its opening for the day.

Just standing outside that ride, the scent of motor grease and old wood rose up on the slightest breeze. The excitement mounted as we heard the clack, clack, clack of the cars as they began the journey through the doors of the old spook house.

There was a jungle cruise around the back of the park where a large pontoon boat floated through murky green water and large realistic-looking animals would scare and delight us.

Mom and Dad mostly played a roll-a-ball game called Fascination, a bingo-type of lighted board game where they won countless tickets that gave out amazing prizes.

When we returned to the hotel at the end of a long day, the old

Victorian décor welcomed us back with atmosphere and charm. There was no air-conditioning, but we caught the heavenly breeze from Conneaut Lake. Sleep would overtake us with the knowledge that we had one more day to spend in the park. One more day to make memories that would last a lifetime.

My Baby Brother Rick and Dad

CHAPTER 17

*H*igh school ended for me in seventy eight. Nono passed away right before I graduated. I grew closer again with Nonna and began to spend a lot more time with her. There were fascinating stories she told of her time in Italy as a little girl; stories of growing up on a farm and being poor; stories of coming to this country and not knowing the language and customs. I loved hearing about her father because in many ways, he sounded just like mine: a good, quiet man with a big heart.

Nonna was an amazingly strong woman for her age and still cooked, baked, and gardened. She had a hearty laugh and still sang while she worked. Though she needed help writing out cards and letters and shopping for groceries, I never minded doing so. It was precious time with a woman who had done so much for me as a child.

I was faced with the decision of what to do with my life though. I completed a nine month course of business school, but my heart wasn't truly in it. I wanted to be a helper, but what . . . where?

My mother had been browsing the newspaper Want Ads. "Kar," she said. "Look at this. It says 'Dental Assistant: will train.' I wonder if that's something you'd like to do."

"I don't know anything about that," I said. But upon checking the phone number that was supplied, we found it was my own dentist, Dr. Alvin Zamba who was looking for help.

"It couldn't hurt to call," Mom said.

An interview was set. Though the dentist I interviewed with was a new graduate and would be Dr. Zamba's associate, I still liked him immediately. I was hired and went through a period of on-the-job-training. But I remember a few duties were almost too much for me.

The day I first assisted for oral surgery, I almost quit. There was blood in the patient's mouth—lots of it. I hadn't signed up for this. As a compassionate sort, I felt as if we were hurting the patient. I had to leave the room.

I worked with a lady who ran our front desk, Kay. She saw me leave the room and must have seen the look on my face. Kay was kind, but she also was very blunt.

"What's the matter?" she asked.

"I can't do this," I said. "I feel so bad for that man in the chair. It seems like we are hurting him."

"Now look," Kay said. "That patient is completely numb. He doesn't feel a thing. You are the one who is feeling, and that's not a bad thing. But I want you to get back in there and realize that you are helping him by what you are doing. If he doesn't have this procedure done, there would be all sorts of infection in his mouth."

I took a deep breath and also took to heart the words that my co-worker said. I am a helper. Yes, I liked those words. I could do this after all. I went back to the doctor's side, and helped him finish the surgery. Those types of procedures never bothered me again.

I loved working in the dental field. Our patients became dear to me, and I always treated them kindly. I felt as if I made a difference in their lives by listening to their stories, and then helping take care of their oral health. Though the young dentist moved on to his own practice in another town after a few years, I ended up staying behind with Dr. Zamba. It got to the point that I could almost read his mind on anything he needed for our patient care. He was fair, a good man, and a great teacher, though quiet. And since I wasn't very quiet, I loved chatting with our patients when they first entered our office. I did everything I could to make them feel warm and welcomed.

Life was indeed the most normal for me during this time. I was nineteen and had everything I needed. Everything except a strong relationship with a boyfriend.

CHAPTER 18

*H*igh school years were the most fun I'd ever had with relationships. I'd learned to wear a little makeup and get pretty haircuts. I bought books that helped me learn to get over shyness and insecurity. I dated several guys from school through the years, gone to proms and Christmas dances and felt like the belle of the ball.

Boys became my world. I flitted from one relationship to the other, though some of them were a little more serious for a time. I became known as the girl with the pretty smile or laugh. My mother used to tell me that my smile brightened my whole personality and looks. And did I smile!

When high school ended though, many of the boys I knew went on to colleges in other towns or states. Where would I find possible marriage material? For wasn't that what I was supposed to be training for now? Marriage? If I had thought it out, I would have taken my time. But I rushed headlong into a very serious relationship with a young man from another town. A man I eventually married when I was only twenty years old.

He was perfect—handsome and funny. We grew close right away. He was in his twenties: a man who could charm anyone with his wit and humor and a laugh that could warm the chilliest heart. There wasn't anyone who disliked him. People took notice of his zany antics, good looks and charming ways. His heart seemed big, his kindness evident, and sense of compassion, great. He fell in love with me and my family. He adored them and the way they made him feel: welcomed and loved; a true part of them. I, of course, fell deeply in love with him.

We married within a year. Our apartment was tiny, but well-kept, clean and cozy. We didn't have much furniture, no rich lavish decorations, but we had each other. Laughter, compassion and goodness continued to be a part of our world. Our lives seemed to be a testimony of love to people we met.

As time went on, the man I married yearned for more. His small world became a prison to him. He wanted a better job, grander things to please him. I wasn't enough for him. I wondered what I could do to keep him happy. Should I change? Would he be more content if I was prettier, skinnier?

Then the day I never dreamed of arrived. He told me our relationship was over. He wanted out of the marriage, out of our small world. He had big places to go and many important things to do. I wouldn't be welcome in this new life he'd chosen. After only three-and-a-half years, he began to pack his bags while I tried to hold onto him. He pried my fingers off, as I sobbed.

I'd noticed the small changes over time. How he began drinking alcohol more. Nights he would head out to work at the late shift at the steel mill and then return the next day to treat me so differently as if he were a stranger. He became angry and indifferent, using vile language that he'd never used before. My heart had broken; there was nothing I could do.

He'd become strangely possessive and jealous and he forbade me to leave our apartment at times. Our phone rang at odd hours and when I picked it up, the caller hung up. I began to wonder.

Just a few months after he left, my friend Goldie called me. "Karen," she said, "I wanted to tell you something before you find out another way."

I braced myself.

"Your ex-husband's picture is in the paper with a new wife. I'm not sure who the girl is. I thought you should know."

I found out that it was a secretary at the place he worked. Some of his late night excursions, phone ringing at odd hours, and secrecy were the two of them skirting around behind my back. All the jealousy he'd held for me was because he was untrustworthy. He took it out on me what he'd been doing for a long while—cheating.

I couldn't eat and dropped a lot of weight at the time. I found myself listless and depressed. I hated myself and knew that I would never be good enough for anyone. This began a lifelong bout of insecurity—of feeling that I would never measure up to anyone. After all the fun of high school and how wonderful I'd felt, I now knew that I'd failed as a wife. Nobody could love me.

To make it worse, we also lost my Nonna at that time. She'd developed a major heart problem and landed in the hospital, never to return home. Sadness overwhelmed me. I would have to face my first great losses that year without my beloved grandmother and also without a husband that I'd adored. It felt like an empty dark hole took the place of where my heart had been.

A young, pretty lady who lived in the apartment downstairs found out that I'd become single. She told me she wanted to help lift me out of my depression. She said she would take me to clubs that had dancing. I had no idea what that entailed, but as I learned how to dress for these places, I began to feel a little bit pretty again. When guys started dancing with me and then asking for my phone number, I reveled in all the attention.

It didn't take long for me to look for love in all the wrong places, however. In many ways I felt I was getting back at my ex-husband. I'd show him who was popular and desired. What I didn't realize was how much I was hurting myself with cheap dates who only wanted one thing. I was using them as I let them use me. It was not a healthy time.

A year later, I met Mark. I'd graduated with him and had known him vaguely in high school. We started dancing together at the club. He was different, kind and sweet. We began a relationship that resulted in a pregnancy. It was the one time I was terrified of my mother. Although I was twenty-six-years-old, I dreaded telling her. I knew she would flip.

My mother berated me and I felt horrible. I was a dirty bad girl and a terrible example to my younger brother. Though it hurt, I vowed I would make it up to her and everyone else. Mark and I decided to get married and "do the right thing."

He had a child out of wedlock already, an eighteen-month-old boy named Josh. He was adorable, but he only wanted his daddy. Though I tried, he wouldn't bond with me.

When our son, Matthew was born, I adored him. I still carried tons of guilt because he wasn't conceived the "right way," but he was mine and he was perfect. I guarded him jealously over his older brother. I felt that Mark's family didn't take to Matthew as they did with Josh, and it became evident to me, who they favored. That hampered my own feelings about him. We still couldn't bond.

I'd read that it wasn't unusual for stepfamilies to take a long time to feel for one another. The fact that I was terribly insecure didn't help. I grew jealous of the attention that I felt was lavished on Josh's mother. I didn't like Mark having to pick up his son at her house.

Of course I felt guilty that I wasn't a loving role model to Josh. I even snapped at him to the point where he once said, "I hate you, Karen."

I was scarred and I was scared. I must be the worst person on earth, I thought. What can I do differently? What could change our relationship? Only time would tell.

The two boys were inseparable, however, as they grew. Watching them together and knowing just how much Matt loved his brother, began to chip away at my hardened heart. Matt was shy and didn't make other friends easily. He loved being with his brother, and Josh became his best friend.

I fell in love with Josh as if he was my own son during that time. I saw him for who he was, so different from Matt, but such a sweet child in his own right. He was bold, courageous, and fun. He had enough energy for three kids. I began to enjoy being mom to both of these boys. Though Josh stayed with us on the weekends and mostly through the summer, I made sure he had everything he needed at our house. He had his own chest of drawers for clothing, toys, and personal items. He was not just a visitor, he was family. I played games with my boys, and we went sledding in our large back yard in the winter. I laughed at their antics in our swimming pool in summer. Life seemed very good for a while.

Matt and Josh

CHAPTER 19

*I*n the early eighties, when I was planning the marriage to my first husband, my father came home one day with a suggestion for my mother. She'd been dabbling a little with antiques, finding unique items at yard sales and second hand stores and re-selling them for profit. Dad wondered if Mom might want to have her own little store.

In our small town of Ambridge, Pennsylvania, there were several Mom and Pop stores that sold the usual staples, such as milk, bread, etc. There was one store located near our town's high school that sold penny candy and other neat things as well as all the regular items.

It was called The Eighth Street Dairy and Mom and Dad took a good look at it when it went up for sale. I'd never pictured them owning a business since my father had a pretty good job at our local post office. Yet it was something he wanted for Mom, he said. So they bought it.

Badly in need of a makeover, the old store looked forlorn and aban-doned. Old insulbrick coated the exterior, and ugly flooring covered the whole place. Shelves needed replaced and stock needed updated. With a little help, my family went to work on it.

They repaired some of the old flooring and then bought carpet remnants at a local store. With different styles and colors of carpet, they made a patchwork design on the floors with the small sections. Everything was scrubbed from top to bottom. Glass cases gleamed; surfaces were completely disinfected. They called an exterminator for a bug problem in the back of the store. Stock was replaced, and several video game machines were brought into the store. An old lunch counter with stools sat off to the side. Dad re-covered the material on the seats and they looked like new.

There was a small table top Kicker/Catcher game where you put in a penny and dropped a small metal "football" for the player to kick to different score levels. One of the video games, Super Astro Fighter became every kid's daily battle. It wasn't unusual to see a group of boys clustered around the machine, cheering for one another to lose so they would keep the highest score.

Mom found unique penny candy that hadn't been previously sold in our area. My aunt, her sister-in-law, sent Gummi Bears from one of their trips to Germany, which quickly caught on in the U.S. Kids went crazy for the soft, colorful candies. Mom even had a few of her antiques for sale.

When high school let out at 2:22, hoards of kids would flock into the newly re-opened store. Mom had small paper sacks filled with one hundred pieces of each candy. She made these during the morning and was able to sell them quickly instead of counting them out one by one.

There was a short time when Mom wanted to do something more special. She had a Crockpot at home, and she began making home-made Sloppy Joe sandwiches to sell at the store. She advertised with a cute, handmade sign of a crudely drawn bun with smoke rising from it, Mom's idea worked. Truckers and other workers stopped in for her delicious sandwiches. She thought it was okay because they weren't cooked in the store, but eventually she had to stop making them due to state regulations.

Dad joined my mother later in the day when he was done with work, or during his lunchtime to help. My brother had fun with the new friends he made at the dairy.

The real magic was in my mother, however. This seemed to be what she was meant to do. I never saw her look more beautiful or happy than during the time she owned that little store. She blossomed and laughed; she made friends with people she never would have met otherwise.

The outpouring of great conversation with the folks that walked through the door was a true strength of my mother. Her face lit up when a good friend or favorite young person walked through the door. She knew when they were having a bad day, and she knew the right words to say.

The best part was that Mom became a true listener. Older people stopped in with nothing else to do. Mom sat them down and gave them her complete attention. Everyone was made to feel special and important under my mother's caring ways. People looked forward to daily visits at the dairy. The air seemed charged with positivity.

School children got to know Mom and even some of the hardest cases—the bullies—fell under the spell of my mother's goodness. Because her own childhood had been so rough, she knew where a lot of these kids were coming from when they told their stories. Her heart of compassion and sensible words began to help people from around the community. She made every person feel they were the only person that mattered in the time she had with them.

One time during the night, our little store got robbed. The cash register was cleaned out and many goods had been stolen. Their huge front picture window was destroyed. I thought my mother might lash out in anger. I wondered if she might think it was too dangerous to continue working there.

Not my mother. She surprised us all. On a large sign that she placed on the front door of the shop, she wrote: **Please do not steal from us. If you are hungry or in need of something, just ask.**

Another time, a group of rowdy teens sat around the side of her building when I came for a visit. I heard them say a few nasty sexual remarks. I told Mom about it. She went outside and said, "If I ever hear of any of you say another thing about my daughter, you'll have to deal with me." The boys apologized and left.

During our time at the Eighth Street Dairy, we made friends with some of the regular customers. Albert was one, and Claude, another. Claude was my age, and I'd remembered going to Kindergarten with him, but then lost sight of him through the years. He was a handsome black fellow with a beautiful smile. Mom and Dad took these two and several other people under their wings. They didn't know their backgrounds or if their lives were happy or not. But I do remember Claude saying one thing to my mother. "If ever I'm in a bind, and about to do something questionable, I always wonder, what would Mrs. Mattia say? It's stopped me from doing a lot of stupid stuff."

My mother had a special place in her heart for Claude, and when he visited town through the years after he'd left, he always made a point to see her again. I felt that many of these folks were like second family.

Mom had a good friend, Norma Jean, who stopped by almost daily. She sat at the counter talking with my mother for hours. They'd known one another when they were younger and now their friendship bloomed even stronger. Norma and Mom laughed like two silly schoolgirls together. Hours passed with their storytelling.

There were also sad people who trudged in with stories of abusive spouses. There were those who had sicknesses that Mom promised to pray for. Mom told the story of her near death experience to many at that time. Our two years at that little store were like a miracle in our lives and a gift to the community. When it came time that they were no longer making a profit, Mom and Dad decided to sell.

On a corner of Duss Avenue and Eighth Street in the small steel town of Ambridge, there was once a place of magic; a place that many could come and share their cares, dreams, hopes, and troubles. There was once a woman and man who made the magic happen. It was more than a building; it was home and a safe haven for many. A place where everyone truly knew your name.

Actual Newspaper Clipping when Mom and Dad Bought the Eighth Street Dairy

CHAPTER 20

*E*ven though I'd been divorced, and re-married, I felt good
about raising my son with loving grandparents. We looked
forward to our visits at their home. My brother and his friends adored
my parents' place as well. There always was a group of about four or
five boys that came to our parents' house. They hung around the basement more than any other place besides being outdoors. It became a
sort-of club house for them, and these young men became like family
to all of us too.

We all congregated at Mom and Dad's through the years for good
conversation and hearty laughter. Mom was a gifted storyteller, and
though I knew some of her tales by heart, they were the first time my
boys or Rick's friends heard them.

Christmas was extra special at Mom and Dad's. Our father always
chose the biggest tree for Mom. We all took turns making it beautiful
with ornaments handed down through the years. Everyone had their
favorites. I loved the ones with glitter and a small faux jewel in the
center.

The same manger scene sat under the tree since I was born. I had
played with the characters, Mary, Joseph, the wise men and shepherds
when I was little. Now I touched them lovingly with nostalgia.

Styrofoam angels stood as sentinels, and a set of old plastic wise men on their camels. Though the legs had broken on some of them, my father cleverly repaired them with pieces of wood and they stood tall again on four legs.

It seemed that every surface in their house was adorned with some sort of old-fashioned glitz from a bygone era. Dad painstakingly placed a little bit of Christmas everywhere. He decorated the windows and outdoors with the old-fashioned lights. You could hear the snap of his staple gun fixing the wires in place. Though the lights were very old, Dad always seemed to find a spare if they burned out. I swear he must have bought tons of them when he was younger.

Mom's Christmas baking was legendary and nobody left their home hungry. She made the traditional Italian cookies, pizzelles, lemon knots, nut horns, and strufali. She made other cookies from a favorite cookbook—one that had so much dried batter on the pages you could have popped it into the oven and baked it that way.

As a bunch of us settled in one Christmas Eve, Mom told a story I'd heard before. "You know," she said, "God sometimes allows angels to visit us on earth but we don't know who they are."

Several pairs of eyes stared as Mom continued. "When I was a little girl, oh, maybe about eight or nine, we always had Christmas Eve dinners over my Aunt Angeline's house. They were big affairs and though we were all poor, there was always tons of food that night.

"We'd finished eating and all the ladies were doing dishes in the kitchen. The men were downstairs drinking and playing an accordion. There was a knock at our door.

"My cousin Walter, who was about my age, went with me to see who it was. Standing outside was a man, a very dirty, poor, and scruffy-looking man.

"He asked if our family would be kind enough to spare him some extra food on this cold night. He was so hungry, you see, and didn't have anything.

"We children ran into the kitchen to tell our parents. They quickly filled up bags of leftovers for the man and he thanked us and we closed the door.

"Walter and I wanted to see where the man had gone. We were

curious if he had a family perhaps too. We opened the door and went out onto the porch. It had been snowing pretty heavily throughout the day, but had stopped a few hours before. But what we saw on the ground amazed us the most. There should have been footprints in the snow from where the man stood and where he walked, but there was nothing. It was as if he vanished into thin air. We ran back in to tell our families, and everyone agreed that we'd encountered an angel that night."

Matt and Josh looked at us with amazement on their faces. Rick's friends looked uncomfortable, but they didn't laugh. None of us could say we'd had such a visit, but hearing my mom re-tell this special story to the next generations became something that would stick with all of us through the years.

Mom was very extroverted. She began calling our local radio station, WMBA and chatting with the host during his "on air" show. It got to the point that he actually looked forward to his conversations with her every day. She told old Italian stories and even was bold enough to sing songs on the air. I'll never forget one time when it was near Thanksgiving, and Mom told me she was going to sing a song she'd learned in school on the radio, "Big Fat Turkey."

I grabbed Matt and Josh, and we huddled near our own little radio at home. The host welcomed Eileen again and asked what she was up to today.

"Well, Dave," Mom said, using the host's name as she always did, "Today I'm going to sing a song for your listeners."

It was quiet for a moment. Then in her deep voice Mom belted out, "There's a big fat turkey out on Grandpa's farm and he thinks he's very gay. He spreads his tail into a great big fan, and he struts around all day. You can hear him gobble at the girls and boys 'cause he thinks he's singing when he makes that noise. But he'll sing a different song that way, upon Thanksgiving Day. . ."

Matt and Josh cracked up. I tried to hold in my own laughter. But minutes after her little tune ended on air, callers began to compliment

Eileen for her wonderful song. Many of them knew the tune and it brought them back to their own childhood.

I think Mom felt like a celebrity in those days—she enjoyed the attention. Once again, however, she just liked reaching out to people and giving them a laugh or good memory.

My father was different. He was an introvert. He seemed happiest being around all of us—his family. He was quiet and strong and his humor was of a different sort. For Dad never stopped inventing make-believe sayings and words. He'd done that since I was little, but it got to the point that everyone, even his co-workers started to speak his special language.

CHAPTER 21

I was called Toy, Toots, and little Tenya. My brother was called Boy and Mattie. My son Matt was Raymond. Others were Fritzie, Nemon, Hage, Johnny Boy, and Rollo. There was Magruter, Ollie, Donelda, Cherley, and Merdet. If my father liked a person, he gave them a special name. It didn't matter that some of the names weren't normal. My father's special language wasn't normal.

When you drank too much pop and left the empty cans around you were a "Socack." When something came crashing down during rough play with your friends you heard, "Save the pieces!" When you wanted someone to leave because you were tired of them, you heard, "Bid it!" (Dad's phrase for Beat it!)

"Flutes" were little kids and not instruments to be played. When you couldn't hear someone speak, you were called "Orville!" And when sneezes came in rapid succession, sounds like "Warf," and "Whoosk" were heard instead of "Achoo."

If you spent too much money on a gift for my dad, he called you "Mike Money or "Andy Mellon." Of course this was said with love because my father enjoyed gifts so much.

Sometimes my father would ask me, "Are you a good witch, or a bad witch?" with his best Billy Burke impersonation from *The Wizard of Oz*. Other times he would make fun of those of us who had computer skills and asked if we went on the "corn.cob" site.

When a person stared at something with big eyes, we heard them called "Beadie Lajolla" or "Heady La Eyeball." If you washed too much you were a "Cleanso Smith." If you preferred to keep secrets you were "Mystero."

Cats did not have whiskers, but they did have "Weeyers." And if Dad wanted a dog or cat to leave him alone he'd shout: "Boorelea!"

Restaurants that truckers frequented were called "Greasette Spoonette" and not Greasy Spoons. That was far too ordinary for Dad. When he saw me wearing shorts in the summer, he called them, "Wearing my diaper." He called winter coats "Buffalo skins." There was no end to the wonderful world of madness and made-up words.

I remember when my brother Rick was little, and Dad wanted him to behave, he would threaten to give his toys away to the mysterious "Francie Blaho." Now Francie was not a real person, but Rick didn't know that, and he would "Straighten up and Fly Right" as Dad would say.

When any child annoyed Dad, he said he was going to turn into "Thrasheto, the Thrashing Monster." Everyone behaved then. This seemed to be worse than Godzilla, Mothra, or any of the old movie creatures.

The biggest word for my father was his greeting: "Henna!" He called that out as he said hello to the guys at work, or upon entering our house each evening. It earned him the nickname of Henna until my son found another name for Dad.

One day, Matt played in the basement near to where my father was trying to clean and reorganize his workshop. Apparently there were a few old broken lamps on his workbench. They were in the way, cluttering his area, and as Dad began rooting through them, he began to shout, "Lamp, lamp, lamp!"

Matt called out, "No, Lamp" instead of Gramps as a name for Dad and it stuck. There were many other wonderful nonsensical sayings, some we never found the origins.

My father lived simply in a quiet place within himself. He was known as shy in many ways but his crazy language stayed with him and us all of his life.

Dad in Funny Hat

Dad and Matt

CHAPTER 22

$\mathcal{I}$t seemed inevitable that anxiety would enter my life at some point. It happened in my late thirties. I started to get stomach aches and shortness of breath. It got to the point that I felt that I couldn't breathe at all sometimes—as if an elephant was sitting on my chest.

One day after all of our patients had gone, the doctor said goodbye as I finished up sterilizing instruments and cleaning the rooms. A wave of terror overwhelmed me, and I could hardly move. There was no way I could leave and get into my car. If I headed out the door, something horrible would happen. I knew that I would smother. At one point, my mother called and asked why I wasn't there for our usual evening dinner. I couldn't explain. Finally, with a leap of faith, I left, hyperventilating. Everything appeared bleak.

After making an appointment and getting checked out by my doctor, I found out that I was experiencing panic or anxiety attacks.

Mark and I had married quickly. I'd sometimes felt as if we should have taken our time and thought things out a little better. Also, his father wasn't an easy man and I sometimes felt like he was trying to control us like a ship with the rudder of his words.

I began to see our differences and realized that we didn't want the same things out of life. I wasn't content watching him play sports on the sidelines any longer. But I'd never felt like I could express my true feelings. I felt smothered at other times. I felt as if my opinions didn't count. Because I was so meek, however, I acted the part of a good little girl and did what I was told. I held down and repressed a ton of feelings. I never spoke unkindly or in defense of myself.

Holding it all in, led me to panic. Repression turned to depression and all sorts of anxiety. It was with a sense of sadness that I told Mark that I wanted out of our marriage.

We had been married about eleven years when I left with our son, Matt, and we went to live with my parents for about a year. Afterward, I found a small house to rent. Though anxiety continued, I finally sought help and began seeing a therapist. There was so much to tell them about my childhood and subsequent failed marriages. Because I was Catholic and had recently felt a true longing for God, I harbored so much guilt.

Before I'd left Mark, something unusual happened in my dental office one evening. It was Christmastime, and I was closing up alone for the night. The white twinkling lights I placed around my desk were still on, and their glow was cozy in the semi-darkness. I sat down in our small reception room and looked around. A beautiful feeling overwhelmed me, a feeling of love so pure that it washed me from my head to my toes. I spoke out loud asking God to give me that beautiful, personal relationship I had only heard about. I was changed. I felt loved.

How odd that I had severe anxiety after experiencing this. It almost seemed dark elements were at work against me, trying to keep me down. It felt as if the enemy was trying to throw me off track and confuse me.

I had never been anywhere but the Catholic Church, but I knew I wanted something more. I began reading my Bible and found passages that pertained directly to me. I sought other churches and listened to uplifting messages. Along with therapy, I began to live the life I thought was best for me.

~

What I hadn't planned on was dating again, and so quickly. As I'd done when my first husband left, I broke free and lived in a way that wasn't healthy. I jumped into relationships and sought comfort from men once again. Because I'd recently wanted to change my life for the better, the terrible guilt continued because I couldn't have it both ways. I despised myself for being weak. Yet I didn't know what to do to make the necessary change.

I felt like a bad mother. I left Matt with my parents as I went on little trips and dates. I stayed up late, started drinking too much, and lived a lifestyle that wasn't really mine.

It was around this time that my first husband contacted me. He said he needed to meet me and get something off of his chest. It was a total shock.

His family and I had lost sight of each other for several years until I saw them at our local mall one day. His father, upon realizing it was me, hugged me and cried. Then soon after that, I got to see my ex sister-in-law, and mother-in-law. We began to pick up the shattered pieces of the life that had been stolen from me so young. I was invited to their homes and treated like family once again. It was more than that—a true deep friendship and understanding developed between us all. I loved them and they, in turn, shared their love with me unselfishly. My early marriage hadn't been in vain.

When I agreed to meet with my ex, years of grief poured out of him. Red-faced and sobbing, he apologized for leaving me behind and hurting me so cruelly. He'd gotten everything he wanted in life: fancy job, huge home, gorgeous women, and mountains of money, yet he'd lost his soul in the process. Would I absolve him, he asked.

I thought back to the simple life we'd once shared; the fact that he'd been the first love of my life. I remembered the ache, the loneliness I'd gone through when he'd first abandoned me. I thought about his anger and cruel words.

He admitted that he'd cheated on me. I heard things that should have pierced my heart, how he'd gotten the secretary pregnant in the office he worked during our marriage, and how she hounded him to leave me.

If it had been any other time in my life, I would have shut down and shut him out. However, I absolved him that day. What did I have to lose at this point? We were two different people now. He meant nothing to me. And the fact that I could extend forgiveness to this man who had hurt me so cruelly meant that I could be free of any hold he may have had on my earlier life and how I had felt about myself.

There had been so much insecurity and self-loathing when he first left. I thought I'd never measure up to other women, especially because I'd been the disfigured one—the girl with the curvature of the spine. We parted ways as friends, and though I still carried a little of the burden of insecurity, I felt lighter. Thankfully, his family and I never lost sight of one another again.

CHAPTER 23

$\mathcal{A}$nother venture presented itself to my parents in the nineties. Dad had been able to retire early from the post office, and he devoted his time to helping Mom with another of her heart's desires: to become an antique shop owner.

My mother found a passion in buying old trinkets and re-selling them to people in antique stores. The more she did this, however, the more she longed for her own little shop. Her first venture was a pretty little place on a quiet tree-lined street in the neighboring town of Sewickley. The location was quaint, and the shop, cozy. Mom decorated it with lovely old furniture adorned with lace doilies and trinkets from other eras. A few other people rented spaces from her, and together they made a very sweet antique shop.

Mom was an amazing business person who could hold her own with the best of them. Some of the people in town may have appeared snobbish, but my mother never let that get to her. She ran her place fairly and firmly, but with kindness. She met countless individuals from the area who had unique stories of their own, and people really began to like my mother in the town.

Dad developed a new-found passion as well. In talking with some of the people who frequented their shop, my father began telling them how much he enjoyed refinishing old furniture. There were several pieces throughout the store that he had worked on with care. Now customers began to come to Dad with their own unfinished projects.

Dad set up shop in his garage and like a true tradesman he carefully restored pieces to their original beauty. He worked on fireplace mantles, china cabinets, dining room tables, and many types of chairs. He spent hours at it while Mom ran her little store. Again, my parents had amazed me with their passion and talents.

A few years into their happy venture, Dad developed heart problems. His doctor found that he'd had a silent heart attack, and there were blockages in his arteries—one very serious. He needed open heart surgery and our family was dumbfounded and fearful. My father had spent all of his life avoiding doctors, and now the bill had come due. Dad had to have this done.

When he entered the hospital, a young parish priest came to visit. He had visited our family before at the antique store, and had told them during their conversation that God had blessed him with the gift of healing. It was with complete faith that we called the priest to come and pray for Dad.

After that day, my father seemed content and seemed ready for major surgery. He had to be transferred to a different hospital for the procedure.

Dad had a setback however. It appeared that there was a sac of fluid encasing his heart. My father had been a heavy smoker most of his life. The doctor cautioned that it was the smoking that had caused this problem and they couldn't proceed with surgery unless they could get rid of the fluid sac.

The outcome appeared grim and unsure. Medications were given to my father and didn't seem to be working. One of the nurses told me that they might have to send Dad home with us to live out his final days in peace. I think God had other plans.

Miraculously, the fluid sac finally began to abate. Dad's surgery was rescheduled, and with many dear friends, me, my mom, and my brother sat and waited some of the longest hours of our lives.

∾

When Dad returned home after a lengthy hospital stay, our family fretted and fussed over him as if he was a child. We had read that some people have a definite change in behavior after open heart surgery and that sometimes they may become depressed or have terrible nightmares.

It took a while for me to believe that my father wasn't going to break into two pieces. With good physical therapy and answered prayers, he did better than everyone expected. Though one of his bypasses was a bit sketchy in his quadruple surgery, the functioning three grafts were quite successful. Dad also quit smoking which was a true miracle.

When he was able, my father began to take small walks outside his home. As his healing progressed further, I met him for longer daily walks. These are some of the most special times I spent with my dad. We walked several blocks in his neighborhood and spoke of the flowers, shrubs, and decorations that bordered the lovely homes. Bird activity enthralled us, squirrels, rabbits, and chipmunks entertained. We talked of life, and my job, family, and what Dad could do instead of the hard work of refinishing furniture.

As it turned out, this became the time that my father began to make small crafts. We set up a workshop in my brother's old bedroom and started buying all sorts of things for him. Word search books, Balsa wood airplane kits, nature puzzles, and finally dollhouse kits. Dad became so good at making those pretty little homes, that he gave some away and sold others. He thrived by staying busy.

Though our parent's days in business together were over, it didn't seem to bother them as much as I thought.

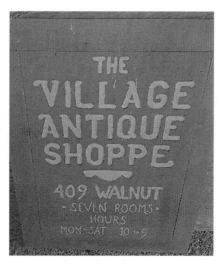

Actual Sign of Mom's Antique Shop

CHAPTER 24

I had to have a minor outpatient procedure done that required anesthesia. I'd been frightened of surgery ever since my time at Children's Hospital when I was young. But everything went well, and there were no complications. But then I received a phone call at work.

"We need you to come in for an x-ray. There appears to be a spot on your lungs."

I clicked off the portable phone with shaking hands. The dentist looked at me across the patient we'd been working on. As the only employee, dental assistant and receptionist, my duties were numerous. I knew that my boss didn't like me to get personal calls. But I think he could tell by the look on my face that it was something very serious.

Fear grabbed hold of me. I had no words. I had to finish the patient's procedure while my stomach cramped and clenched with terror. I tried not to let my hands shake as we continued working.

I imagined the worst right away. I'd always been a glass-half-empty sort-of person. News always meant something bad. But this—a spot on my lung. It had to be cancer.

So many thoughts roiled within me at once. *I'm only thirty-eight. My son is ten. I can't leave him now. He needs me. What about my parents? We were such a close family. What would this do to them?*

After we dismissed the patient, I told my boss about the phone call. I excused myself from the office for the rest of the day. I had to find answers.

I drove three blocks to my physician's office. I barely noticed the brilliant hues of the red and gold fall leaves on the trees lining the streets. People walking along the sidewalks blurred as tears stung my eyes. Though Thanksgiving would soon be approaching, I had nothing to be thankful about.

When I walked into the doctor's office and informed the receptionist I was there, she told me to wait a few minutes and they would call me back shortly. I tried picking up a magazine to browse through or tried smiling at the others seated nearby. Nothing worked. I could feel fear choking me.

New x-rays were taken and I waited for the doctor in an examination room. It didn't take long for him to bring in the new films.

"Here it is," he pointed out. "A spot on your left lung." He compared it to the x-rays taken one month before.

The words hung in the air until I had the courage to ask, "What can it be, doctor?"

"Well," he said, "it could be an old scar from pneumonia you may have had at one time, or it could be cancer."

Cancer: a word that changes lives. It would certainly change mine.

I left his office that afternoon completely baffled and fearful. Further tests would have to be scheduled.

I called my mother that night. "First of all, I refuse to believe this," she said. "Also your doctor was too harsh. I want you to have a second opinion, honey. I'd like you to see my doctor. She's good and also very compassionate." Mom also spoke with the priest who had prayed with Dad and he agreed to see me right away.

Though I'd been a bit skeptical as I waited for further tests, I knocked on the door of the pastor's small home. He invited me in, and we sat and chatted for a while. Pictures of Jesus hung on the wood-paneled walls: Jesus comforting little children and the sick. *Jesus, please comfort me too,* I thought. Bibles and inspirational reference books lined bookshelves. A sense of peace enveloped me.

I wanted to clear my conscience before he prayed. There were issues that recently bothered me and had given me great guilt. As I spoke, I felt cleansed and a sense of great relief.

He anointed my forehead with spice scented oil that reminded me of the incense our church used during special seasons. He placed his hands on my head as he prayed, and I could feel the depth and power of the healing words as he spoke. There seemed to be a warm sensation going from his hands right through me. When he was done, I thanked him. He asked me to stay in touch.

During the time I had to wait for the scheduled tests, I kept busy with something I enjoyed: raking fall leaves into huge piles on a crisp afternoon. My mind felt free in the fresh air. I'd been reading my Bible daily like a warrior getting ready for battle. I prayed bolder prayers and began to think a bit more positively. The fear that had engulfed me was replaced by a sense of calmness. The touch of the pastor's hands had given me hope.

My mother's doctor met us at the local hospital the day of my tests. She was a tiny lady with a big personality. "I'm going to stay around," she said to me and Mom. "I want to see the results of the scan immediately."

Afterward, when we sat in the waiting area, my mother's doctor came into the room with a perplexed, but cheerful expression. "I don't know what the other doctor saw," she said. "There is absolutely nothing on your scans."

Relief flooded me. Mom and I thanked her for the wonderful news as we hugged one another and cried happy tears.

Later that night as I was praying, I remembered something that my dear friend Mary had said to me a few months earlier. She had called me one day and said, "Karen, I don't know why you are supposed to hear these particular words, but God said everything is going to be okay."

They had been cryptic, but comforting words at the time, and as I thanked my heavenly father that evening, it came to me: I'd already been healed from that moment.

It was easier to think positively as time went on because I'd become a more powerful prayer warrior. When others had issues in their lives, I gave them Bible passages that had comforted me during my own fearful time. I shared my story to bless others. Scriptures were no longer words but living truth.

I stayed in touch with the pastor until he was transferred from our parish and we wrote to each other for a short time. Our family would never forget the special priest with the gift of healing.

CHAPTER 25

Though some people might have thought it a little odd that our family was so close, it never bothered any of us. My parents' house became a gathering place. Matt, my brother and I were always there.

Mom made hearty meals every night for dinner. Matt and I only lived a few blocks from my parent's house, and after his school day, or my work, we headed over for spaghetti, tasty roasts, incredible meat loaf, and homemade pizza or breads. That wasn't our only reason though.

There was hearty laughter and constant ribbing between Matt and his "Lamp," my father. They were so much alike in their actions. Lamp had been good to Matt especially in the time after my marriage failed. It hadn't been easy for my son to make friends through the years since he was extremely shy. But time spent with his grandfather was special as they built fortresses out of blocks when he was little, and made items out of clay when he was older. They'd always played Atari video games together. They took long walks and looked for small "treasures" on the ground. They came back with the simplest items as if they were gold: pencils, erasers, coins, and inexpensive broken jewelry. As Matt got older, they talked together about jobs and everything under the sun. Matt had a small video camera and began filming family events.

I was fortunate to have stayed close with Josh too. Mark knew how much I loved him and how close we had gotten through the years. There were times that Josh came and spent the day with me and Matt.

My brother and I had a great relationship too. Though fourteen years separated us, we confided in one another, laughed together, and commiserated over our parents getting older.

Rick and I worried about Dad ever since the heart surgery. Our father had always been the type of man who could do anything. We looked to him as a super hero and called him for any jobs in our homes, large or small. Now the tables turned drastically and we found ourselves doing everything for him. Dad, who had always been the rock, strength, and hardest worker in our family; Dad, the one who came to our houses to paint, fix gutters and windows. The man who taught me how to mow grass, trim hedges, and prune small bushes by guiding me with his words and the rubber end of his cane as he pointed and said, "You missed a spot." Now we were faced with doing hard tasks for him. We both stepped into this role willingly. Our father had always been so good and loving. Though he never said the words: *I love you*, we knew he did.

Neither parent was overly affectionate. Words were written in cards through the years and I accepted their love and returned it in similar fashion. We didn't hug and kiss, though many Italians are known for that. It was in how we treated one another and how we spoke and listened that we shared the love we couldn't show by touching.

Mom was special, compassionate and heartfelt. She loved her dogs, cats, and all living creatures. When one of them showed signs of sickness, Mom laid her hands on them and prayed for healing. We saw miraculous events through the years. Cats that looked as if they'd used up the last of their nine lives, recovered under my mother's special gift. We saw a beautiful goldfish that had been belly up in the tank for a while restored after Mom held it lovingly and prayed. Though her fingers began to bend with arthritis, the beauty and warmth of her touch always remained the miracle.

My mother felt pain unlike other people. She saw things on television and in life that broke her heart. That tender little girl inside of her, who never had a chance to blossom until she was older, showed the love she'd never been given to every living creature. Her empathy brought her to tears many times, and would be something I wished she didn't have so strongly. Seeing my mother crying would always break my heart.

I remember one time when a bird's nest blew down in her back yard after a big storm and all the babies were lost, the mother bird came to the same branch daily, calling out for them. Mom sat nearby shedding her own tears with the mother bird, talking sweetly to her.

Mom was a child at heart and loved telling stories. She adored Halloween most of all, and in the "spirit" of things, would dress up sometimes as she handed out treats to the kids. She always purchased several bags of the really good candy bars to give away, but some of it would end up in her belly days before, and we'd have to buy new ones by the time Halloween rolled around.

Mom also helped orchestrate our elaborate sets: small graveyards, realistic scary dummies, and spooky music. I remember countless little children who seemed too afraid to come to Mom's porch for their candy, until she or my son would unmask and take the time to show them that the decorations weren't real or that a tape recorder was hidden under a bush nearby piping the screeching sounds into the night.

Mom always sat outside in nicer autumn weather with a bowl of candy balanced on her lap as she greeted each child with a smile and a "Happy Halloween." She always topped the evening off watching one of her favorite horror movies and possibly sharing a creepy story or two with all of us.

My parents' house was the hub for many of our friends to gather through the years since the connecting roads and houses sat fairly close and walking always felt safe in the neighborhood. There seemed to be something magical on Halloween nights. The air was scented with the warm cooking scent of jack-o-lanterns lit with the small stubs of candles on neighbor's porches. Then there was the crunchy wonderful sound of fallen leaves underfoot.

A few times my brother and his group of friends made an elaborate haunted house in my parents' basement, more for themselves than to really scare anybody else. They hung large black plastic sheets from the ceiling to distinguish each area. Every part of the cellar had props and was dimly lit. One area was made up with scary clowns; another, with oozing eyeballs on a plate. A werewolf and organ with bloody fingerprints completed the tour. A local girl, who was a friend of theirs, actually got scared as she walked through.

Sometimes I thought we were more like a group of crazy friends than family. And none of us had ever lived very far from each other. That was about to change.

Halloween at Mom and Dad's House

Rick, Mom, Me, and Dad

CHAPTER 26

*A*fter a few failed relationships, I seriously asked myself, "What is it that I am looking for?" I didn't do well on my own. I wanted a good, strong marriage so badly. There were only so many of the same guys in my area, and I didn't want to go to bars or clubs any longer in other towns. My brother told me about internet dating. It was quite new in the early 2000's. So the girl who barely knew how to use a computer put up a profile and began chatting regularly.

One of the main things on my page besides finding a man who was a Christian believer, was the fact that I would not relocate for anyone. I could never leave my parents or brother.

It was on a site called American Singles (which sounds like some type of cheese, I realize), that I met a man from a town near Pittsburgh. Jim was funny, bold, realistic, and unusual. He was every bit as Italian as me, and his priorities in life lined up with mine. He had two grown children, a daughter and son, who were the same ages as Matt and Josh, around 18 & 21. I liked him right away. We began corresponding and then finally met at a restaurant in a mutually distant place.

Jim loved God, which was a big part of what I wanted in a man. He'd just come out of a failed marriage so I wanted to take it very slowly. He visited me every couple weeks for a while, but then as it became more difficult to be apart, we wondered if we should take our relationship to the next level. I missed him so much when he wasn't around. Because he lived about an hour away, it wasn't easy to spend time with one another.

When a year went by, Jim asked me to marry him and move to Monroeville to his house. Of course I said no right away. "I can't leave my parents," I told him. "They're getting up in age now. They need me."

I did something I'd never done before with any relationship. I began to pray in earnest about the situation, trusting God for the outcome. Signposts began popping up in the form of small scriptures and inspirational messages I read in my Bible or books pointing the way for me. The Genesis: 1 Bible passage *Leave your country, your people, and your father's household and go into the land I will show you* kept appearing everywhere. But what was I to do?

When I spoke with Matt, he told me he would not move. He had begun college and wasn't going to move farther away. He didn't care what I did, but that was that. My brother wasn't happy at all, and my parents seemed to want only my happiness as they always did. Perhaps I was making the biggest mistake of my life, but I made the decision to marry Jim and move an hour away from family. I learned big city driving in a hurry so that I would be able to visit back home every week. The small town girl grew up and began a new life.

Matt stayed with my brother in a small house Rick had just purchased. Though I missed my son terribly, I saw him begin to blossom in ways I may not have seen earlier. He began to cast off his shyness; he started driving to places he never would have gone. There came a time that my son thanked me for leaving our town because he said we both needed to grow. I felt content that I had chosen the best of both worlds.

I found it scary when looking for a new job. After all, I'd worked twenty-seven years for the same dentist in our small town of Ambridge. It was difficult leaving the man who had given me such a great opportunity and training. Dr. Zamba was like family to me, and

I'd grown very close to our patients. He gave me a glowing recommendation letter that landed me a job in a dental office twenty minutes away from Monroeville. In this new office I learned proficient computer skills, and made some of the best friends of my later years.

Though I'd cried at first every morning on my way to the new job, missing my family, Matt, and the old office, as time passed, the new normal felt empowering and good.

Husband Jim and Me

CHAPTER 27

*J*im and I found a great church family after searching for while. We settled with a place that was called Pittsburgh East Community Church. I had never been in such a venue with a stage, Christian rock music, and totally modern messages that shared older Bible stories in a new light. It was everything I had wanted. We joined small Bible study groups and became greeters on Sunday mornings. There were many people in a small circle that we grew close with. Our lives changed and we began to pray together at mealtimes and before we left for work each morning.

It saddened me, however, that Jim had a binge drinking problem I'd not known about. When I was at work and he had a day off without me, he began drinking beer around noon or so as he did household chores. By the time I returned home at night, he was inebriated, and became belligerent when questioned. I had never been around this sort of behavior before, and I didn't handle it well by screaming at him and badgering him. Though I didn't see it often, his actions at our home gatherings also began to give me pause. When my father noticed it one day, it sickened me.

"Uh, Kar," Dad said. "You and I don't pull any punches with each other, right?"

"No," I said on the other end of the phone.

"I didn't like how Peppay (his name for Jim) was talking to you the other day at your house. I don't want that kind of behavior around you."

I sighed. Dad's words had cut me deep. I promised I would talk with Jim.

~

When I had time off from work, and I was in my house alone, I reached out to God with questions. "Lord, you brought me out here. You gave Jim to me, I'm sure of it. What is the meaning of this drinking problem? I don't want it. I don't need it. Please take it away."

Promises were made and not kept by my husband. Though the majority of our time together was wonderful, it was the occasional bouts of binge drinking that gave me such pause and emotional instability.

~

It was about three years into our marriage, around 2009 that I was rocking on our outdoor wicker swing. It is a favorite place of mine, a peaceful respite in nature. Cardinals, blue jays, even a red-bellied woodpecker took turns at the bird feeder nearby. Calmness washed over me when an inner voice spoke very clearly: *Enjoy time with your mother*, it said. Now darkness crept in and blotted out the sun that had been shining brightly in my soul a moment before. *My goodness, does this mean my mother is going to die soon*, I wondered?

I heeded the voice and spent as much time with Mom as I could. I fretted over her health and treated her like a queen. I took her and Dad to the local casino once a month even though I didn't enjoy it. I bought her special foods that she liked and took her out to eat often. I called her constantly to talk on the phone and prayed nothing bad would happen.

~

Through the first years of my marriage, Dad's health was good, though he had occasional bouts of congestive heart failure which came upon him every so often. We would call it a good year if Dad didn't go into the hospital. But as time passed, he had more and more of these episodes. My brother and I made sure to keep Dad busy with the things he enjoyed. We encouraged him to continue making the craft projects he loved so much. Even when we were fearful, it never showed around our father.

My father exuded peace and goodness. He was content to sit outdoors quietly with family. He always said he never needed much. He wore clothes for the longest time until they became ripped or so paint splattered that he finally gave them up. He'd never wanted to travel, and found pleasure in simple everyday tasks.

Dad had a well-worn prayer book that he took outside in the early morning to read. He talked with me sometimes about his faith and asked questions about the Bible.

Dad also loved to eat. He enjoyed meals and snacks. Because Mom was a good cook, he always ate well. He bought little treats for himself like animal crackers, fig bars, marshmallow peeps, and graham crackers. He enjoyed candy and always had a Tootsie Roll stuck to his upper denture.

I invited Dad to stay with me and Jim one weekend. Mom didn't want to come, so we picked up my father and brought him to our house. As we sat outdoors on our side porch, Dad opened up to us. He told stories I'd never heard before—stories about the many girls who'd liked him while growing up, and how shy he'd been. My father was always a handsome man and had been told that all his life. But he'd never understood much about dating and had kept to himself.

I couldn't believe he told us. It was such a sweet story told in an innocent way. As always, it was something that made me love him even more. He made us promise never to tell Mom or my brother.

My father never acted as if he was giving up. He used to say that he was going to live life to the fullest and do what he liked. He said he would never die in a rocking chair, afraid.

But then Dad needed another surgery. His heart doctor decided that a defibrillator/pacemaker would give him a better quality of life. So in his seventies, he had the procedure done. He came through very well. It seemed that nothing frightened him; nothing but worry over my mother.

CHAPTER 28

*W*hy was the computer baffling Mom so much? She played in several gaming sites for the longest time and even talked with people in the chat rooms. I'd been so impressed with her computer skills. She seemed to know much more than me.

When her passwords weren't working, she began blaming my brother. Mom accused him of stealing her sites and using them himself. They bickered so much that Dad began to tell us all to agree with her just to keep her calm.

It was an old trick of my father's—this agreeing game. I'd learned it well when I was little when my mother had mental illness. It began to prey on my mind that we were doing it again. What was going on?

Matt wrote out passwords for her and taped them near her computer. At first, this worked wonderfully. Then she would forget that the notes were even there.

Odder still, dinners began to have weird flavors, or Mom's baking seemed off. Cakes that used to rise high and fluffy were flat and taste-less. Mom blamed old ingredients and bought several boxes of baking powder, baking soda, and extra bags of flour. Kitchen drawers were bulging with extra baking supplies. Why did she have so many of them?

Dad said it seemed like Mom was forgetting what she already purchased when they shopped together. He tried to tell her she didn't need the stuff but she fought with him about it. Her cupboards were full of similar items. Her freezer was packed tightly with extra meat. None of us had ever seen her so excited about shopping before.

~

Enough strange events were happening that I mentioned to my mother's doctor (who was also my doctor), that maybe she was becoming forgetful. He agreed to give her a few small memory tests which she passed at the time.

I couldn't help but become concerned, however, over the difference in Mom's behavior. She snapped more at all of us. When she watched an old movie on television, she became angry and yelled at us if we were making noise anywhere nearby. She'd never done that before, and actually should have known these movies by heart for how many times she watched them. Why was she so bitter all of a sudden? Everything began to annoy her. She even seemed to lose her sweet sense of humor.

Then she asked a lot of questions—ones that didn't seem to make sense. She forgot certain people's names that she'd known well. She wrote things down, but later wondered what she'd meant by the hastily scribbled note. She lost her glasses and partial denture over and over. She blamed the dog for stealing them. We used to chuckle picturing a big husky with glasses and dentures.

She read paperwork as if seeing it for the first time. I was beginning to understand what the voice I'd heard that day on my swing meant: I was losing my mom a little at a time. The woman who had gone through hell and had a glimpse of heaven. Her mind was beginning to falter but in a different way now. It appeared that Mom was developing Alzheimer's.

CHAPTER 29

here was a basket sitting on Mom and Dad's kitchen table that held old receipts, key chains, grocery lists, and a few love notes my father had written to Mom through the years. She had taken some of them out of her bedroom drawer, stuffed them into the basket and read them at the table. They made her blush and giggle. When I visited, she would ask me in a shy, schoolgirl way, "Kar, did you ever see some of the notes your father wrote me?"

Of course I had seen them and now I was seeing them on a weekly basis. Dad sat at the other side of the table and rolled his eyes when Mom wasn't looking. I didn't mind hearing the notes read again. They bespoke of true love.

A special Merry Christmas to the one I adore. You are the true meaning of Christmas. I wish to thank you for everything you've given to me. I know you've had to struggle your whole life. You've had a wealth of good feelings for everyone. God Bless, All my love, Rich . . .

Good morning honey. I love you. Hope you had a good rest and sleep. Thanks for being so good, nice, and thoughtful to me. I love you so much for that and all our wonderful life together. Stay always with me. I need you. With all the love in the world, Love, Rich . . .

Dear Honey, Just a few lines to let you know that I care for you. Although

I may not show you often, I really need you, want to love you, and want to make you happy. You mean everything to me. Share your burdens with me, share your love with me, share your whole life with me. God only knows the joy and happiness you've given to me. We all have ups and downs some days. Here's hoping that it will be all ups forever. All the love in the world to you. Love from Rich . . .

Things I want you to know: If I were to do it all over again I would pick you. You bring more love into the world than anyone I ever knew. You are the most unselfish person in the world. I love you so much that it hurts. You deserve the best the world has to offer. I love you because of the way I feel with you—warm, true, heartfelt love. I hope you feel this way for me also. Love forever, Rich . . .

Happy Anniversary My Love! Proud to call you my wife; the only love of my life. We've been through so many things; God's given you angel's wings. I love you more after 41 years; Hope there are never more tears. I love you honey. Thank you for all you have done for me. I hope I can give you at least half back. Love you forever, Rich . . .

Good morning honey: Thank you my honey for everything. I love you so much. You are my one love, my only love-you'll always be. I want your love and happiness for as long as we both have. You mean the whole world to me honey. Thank you for showing me beauty and nature and true love. All my love, Rich . . .

There were so many others, but Mom read her favorites often. If her mind was faltering with Alzheimer's, at least she had these beautiful reminders of the love she and my father shared. That was something that memory loss could not steal from her.

Dad and Mom's Wedding Picture

CHAPTER 30

The more time passed, the more precious our parents became to me and my brother. Age crept up quickly on both of them and began leaving them more childlike than ever. Not knowing how much time we had, we grew closer to both of them.

Dad and I had special phone calls in the mornings. If I was showering and missed his call, I'd hear "Sleepin' huh?" on my answering machine. Then I called him back and he talked about bills he'd received, grocery prices, his outdoor flowerbeds, and food. Eventually our talks turned to Mom. I could tell his heart was breaking for her. He asked if I would begin helping him to write out his bills. I, of course, was glad to do so. He put my name on their accounts and we also signed power of attorney papers in case.

It was almost too much for me to admit that our years together were passing on to the final ones. This close family—these crazy, wonderful, loving parents. I tried thinking about life without either of them, and it stabbed my heart and left an awful emptiness. "Please God," I asked, "let us have quality time together for as long as possible."

I worried which one would pass first. I hated thinking about it, but secretly hoped it would be Mom. How on earth would we deal with her worsening memory loss without Dad? He was her world. He made sure pills were taken, meals were eaten, and he cleaned up when she had her first few episodes of incontinence. He made sure she got safely to bed since she had fallen a few times. Mom walked with a cane, but her walking had become erratic. If he woke in the morning before her, Dad made sure to help her out of bed when she awoke. He made her coffee each day and bought her favorite jelly doughnuts several times a week.

When I visited, I began to throw every ounce of myself into our time. I did whatever outdoor work Dad needed, digging flowerbeds, weeding, and general cleanup. I took both of them to doctor appointments. I helped write their bills and took Dad grocery shopping. It was special one-on-one time when we went to the store together. Mom didn't enjoy it so much anymore, but Dad loved to take his time and look at items and prices. "Look, Kar," he would say. "Darn price of o.j. is a lot higher in this store." Or, "Huh, I better buy these bananas because they'll never be that cheap again."

He also walked with a cane and had such a soft-spoken way about him. I held onto his arm sometimes when we walked and people smiled when they saw us together. He became hard of hearing and I translated for him wherever we went.

I loved taking my parents out to eat at favorite restaurants. My son would sometimes join us, and I saw his kindness toward his aging grandparents. He was giving back all that they had done for him in his actions and words. Though he became busy with a YouTube channel he'd begun, and it had gotten very popular, he still made time for them.

My home life began getting to me. I had extra duties with my parents and couldn't handle my husband's drinking when it was out of control. I'd been praying in earnest for years. When he left for work, I sometimes got down onto my knees. I asked God to help me to be a good wife, but also to cause a miracle to happen that would change him. He loved God with his whole heart, but he seemed powerless in overcoming his drinking urges.

Christmas of 2015 was approaching. I had a little family gathering lined up with Jim's children a week before. I told God that it had been too much lately. My parent's failing health, Mom's dementia . . . I needed Jim to change or I might not be able to stay with him.

The night of the party, my husband had a terrible fall outdoors. He ended up in the hospital. Though I felt pity, I also felt that I had my answer. He couldn't or wouldn't change. It would only get worse from there.

When he came home, my husband showed true remorse. *We've been through that before,* I thought. But perhaps I saw something different this time.

Jim made up his mind that he was going to quit drinking. I wanted to believe it. I prayed as never before, and we prayed strongly together about it as well. Time began to pass, slowly at first, and then several months went by and he hadn't had a drink. I remember telling my father by the spring of 2016 that "Peppay" had quit drinking for good. Dad was so proud of him.

Jim was as good as his word. We traveled to places that we loved so well. We began to enjoy new things on our trips with a life that didn't involve alcohol any longer. His life became a testimony to the incredible power of prayer.

CHAPTER 31

*J*anuary of 2016 brought a major health setback for Mom. She began to have rectal bleeding through the night. Rick and Dad called an ambulance and she was rushed to the hospital. It was one of the most difficult parts of our family's journey. First of all, Mom didn't understand what was going on. She forgot everything that was said to her by any doctors or nurses. One of us had to be with her at all times. I knew it was wearing on my dad though. He started to look older to me almost overnight.

When the doctors wanted Mom to have a colonoscopy, I actually fought against it at first. How on earth were we going to get her to drink that bottle of liquid the night before? How would she fare with not being able to eat? I stayed with Mom until very late that night. It was not easy. Fortunately, she had a wonderful male nurse, Matt, who had the patience of a saint with her. He told me to go home and that he would continue to watch out for her personally. He said he didn't have many patients that night and he would give her top priority.

I was able to leave, but Dad and I returned extra early the next day. Her tests turned out well and her gastrointestinal issue was okay. The bleeding could have been caused by a number of other things.

We thanked that kind male nurse, and even Mom didn't forget him.

It was the one thing that stuck out in her mind, and she made sure to bake cookies for him after she returned home.

～

The summer of 2016 brought about a few changes for Dad. First of all, he told me he didn't want to drive any longer. He was eighty-five-years-old, and he said that it was scaring him when he drove to places alone. I was shocked because I wondered how long he would actually want to drive. My brother and I had begun to think about having "the talk" with him.

Then Dad said that the belt on his pants was bothering him. I wondered if he had gained a little weight and thought a bigger belt might be necessary. Though we tried that, he insisted it was still hurting, so I thought suspenders might help and they seemed to give him a bit of relief.

～

There was a prayer that I'd felt had gone unanswered. It was one that involved my dad. I'd been praying for the longest time that God would bestow monetary favor on Dad to get some much-needed things done in his house. The house was showing its own signs of slowing down. Old, rotted wooden windows, peeling paint, and a shower that had been caving in for several years. My parents had struggled financially for a while, and I wondered if God had turned a deaf ear on this particular prayer.

I asked around. Did anyone know of someone who could perhaps help? Did anyone do this type of work for a good price? I was always told the same answers: either "no," or "well, it will cost you a fortune." Rejected, I would walk away and hope that someone, anyone would step up and give us the guidance needed to help with these jobs.

On my way to work one day I asked, "Lord, I ask that you would let my Dad live to see goodness, favor, and blessing on his house. It has been such a tremendous worry for him. I pray for a miracle to occur."

Though Dad and my brother tried their best as the shower wall caved in a little more, I worried that it was unsafe and unhealthy.

My brother had begun to drive Dad to church each Sunday and then pick him up afterward. Our father came home with a paper bulletin in his hand. "Kar," he asked me, "what do you think this means? Catholic Youth Heart Camp. Do you think it's something for heart patients?"

I read over the paragraphs and my eyes widened as I saw all of the jobs the youth camp did. There appeared to be nothing they wouldn't tackle. We called the contact number the following day and found out it was true. If a family was in particular need, they could sign up to have work done around their house, inside and out. I filled out paperwork, answered questions, and got Mom and Dad's house on the list immediately.

The nicest group of young people I'd ever met showed up with their adult mentor. I found their positive attitudes refreshing. It seemed there was nothing they wouldn't be able to do and that included fixing the shower.

I began crying in front of the group of seven young people and their leader. They were an answer to the prayer I'd prayed for so long. God had sent this group to our family at just the right moment. Not early, but certainly not late.

My parents were in awe of the kindness of the teenagers. We found out that these young people give up a week of summer, raising their own money for a time of prayer, reflection, and very hard work. They never grumbled or complained but worked heartily side by side.

Catholic Youth Heart Camp appeared to be the answer to that long-awaited prayer. They worked for free, and fixed my parent's bathroom which had been falling apart. They completely rebuilt the shower area that had caved in and placed new walls around it. They re-attached a small overhanging roof over a back stoop, painted all the outdoor windows, which had weathered and been peeling badly. They repaired the garage roof and did a few smaller jobs as well.

My mother didn't understand why they didn't get paid. Every day when the teenagers showed up, she fretted and fussed over lunch for them. She bought sandwiches or made them herself. It appeared that her kindness came back in a major way with her later dementia. We were certainly blessed as the summer progressed.

～

About this time I'd been sitting on my back porch doing a little writing. I'd recently sold an article to Guidepost Magazine and had been thrilled. A secret passion of mine since childhood was to be a writer. With the vivid imagination I'd had, I wanted to get those stories out of my head and onto paper.

I looked over at my railing and saw a vibrant red male cardinal sitting there. He chirped and studied me with that sideways view that birds have. I began talking to him. "Hello there," I said. "What a pretty birdie you are. Are you hungry? I'll get you something."

The cardinal never moved. He appeared to enjoy the sound of my voice. I went inside and brought the bag of bird seed out. I shook it and placed some in my feeder. The cardinal didn't act frightened of me at all. He landed only a few feet away from me.

This began to occur almost daily. Even when I got out of my car at work each night, that male cardinal would swoop down lower from whatever tree he'd been in, and land close to me as if waiting for me to talk and bring out some fresh seeds.

His birdsong was glorious in the mornings. When I sat on my couch near our big picture window, he would be right in the large bush outside singing his heart out as if the song was just for me. I felt as if we had a special relationship so I decided to call to him as he sat on a branch in my front yard tree. I placed seeds on the flat feeder I had and told him to "come on." He would land, and this time he was only inches from me. I had no idea that to some people cardinals carried special meaning and that they believed them to be angels or spirits of deceased loved ones.

My Special Cardinal

CHAPTER 32

$\mathcal{I}$n early August of that same summer, I received a phone call from my brother. It wasn't usual for him to call me in the early morning, so I always worried that something might be up with Mom or Dad. I wasn't wrong. Rick was on his way to take our dad to the emergency room. When I asked if it was congestive heart failure, Rick told me, no, it was something with Dad's stomach.

I had already gone to work, so I told my boss and co-workers that I needed to leave. They had been used to me doing that for a while, since both parents' health had been failing. It had gotten to the point that every few months, one of them landed in the hospital.

Praying as I drove the hour-and-a-half from my office to Heritage Valley Hospital, I wondered what could be wrong with Dad's stomach. Was this the reason his belt had felt so uncomfortable through the summer? Why didn't he say something sooner if it was bothering him this much?

I made my way into the emergency department. Familiar sights of busy nurses bustling around and familiar sounds of beeping monitors caught my attention before I spotted Dad. He looked good as he lay there with a thin sheet covering him except that his coloring was odd.

Dad's skin was always a little ruddy, but I saw a pale yellowness in his face.

"Hey, what's up?" I asked, eyeing the monitors with Dad's readings behind his bed.

"Ah, my damn stomach kept me up all night," he said. "Got so bad this morning I couldn't move."

We joked around as we'd always done, but I could see that my father was really hurting.

Tests were scheduled and it was found that Dad had gallbladder issues. Of all things it could have been, this was the last malady I would have guessed. Well, it seemed simple enough. Just schedule him for surgery and get the darn thing out.

We all soon learned it wasn't that easy. Dad was put into a regular room at first. He was in such severe pain, he couldn't eat. He doubled over as we chatted, and it hurt me to see him suffering like this. When I brought Mom to visit, she was in her own world. She talked about past stories as if they were still going on, and past loved ones as if they were still here.

It occurred to me that what my father was experiencing wasn't normal. And why were they waiting so long to remove the offensive organ? Doctors came and went. They explained that they were trying some medications and a small procedure on my father due to his age. They were beginning to think that surgery might be risky with his heart history. So we waited a few days but then Dad landed in ICU. I had seen this coming. His coloring was very jaundiced. He hadn't eaten much at all in the three days at the hospital, and his pain level was severe.

I missed a lot of work that week due to keeping an eye on Mom who'd been home without Dad, and running to the hospital to see where things stood. I tried to show up early in the mornings to see my father while I knew Mom was still sleeping.

I stood at Dad's bedside, a gnawing worry eating away at my innards. His monitors seemed stable, his coloring was off, but he was in good spirits when pain medication kicked in. Most every time that Dad had ever been in the hospital, his main concern had always been for my mother. With everything in him, he didn't worry about himself, and usually made light of his conditions. Though the last few days were some of the worst I'd seen him, this morning he wanted to talk.

"Kar," he said. "I saw two people die in my life. My father and an uncle."

"Oh yeah?" I said, wanting to change the subject quickly. A weird feeling came over me, and I wanted to bolt from the room.

A woman doctor walked into dad's cubicle just then. "Good morning, Mr. Mattia," she said. She shook my hand as I explained that I was his daughter.

"Well," she began again, "I'm not sure where we stand. We thought we could take care of things with the small procedure we've done before, but now I'm concerned that the gallbladder could burst and you could become septic.

"It wasn't advisable to have your gallbladder taken out due to your age and history of your heart. Your heart function is only twenty percent. It may not be enough to get you through surgery."

Dad looked frankly at the doctor. He reached over to take my hand and held onto it tightly. I felt a noose of fear tightening my throat. The old tic was back. A knot settled into my stomach.

"So, we have to think about where we stand," the doctor continued. "I'd like to perform the surgery. It may give you a chance. Take your time and think about it. But if we do it, we will be doing it later today."

Dad, ever the gentleman, "Thank you, doctor. We'll think about it."

He looked up at me. "I don't feel *that* sick," he said.

CHAPTER 33

*L*ater that same day, we all gathered at dad's bedside. Me, Rick, and Mom. Dad's heart surgeon came into the room. He was someone who our father liked and trusted.

"Hey, Doc," Dad said. "What do you think about all this?"

The doctor said, "Well, Rich, you have to ask yourself if you are ready to throw in the towel, or if you feel you want to give this a shot."

Mom gasped. It appeared that even she realized the severity of the situation.

"Do I think you can make it through this?" the doctor asked. "Yes. But if you don't have the surgery, sepsis will set in. It could lead to death within a short time. While you have your wits about you, what do you say?" He looked Dad straight in the face. "It may or may not work."

"I want to try the surgery," Dad said.

"Good. I'll have the nurses draw up the paperwork and we will get you ready." He left the room after shaking Dad's hand.

Mom began to cry. I was still in shock from the morning news we'd gotten from the first doctor. I felt I had nothing to offer my mother, no words of comfort. I excused myself and went to the ladies room down the hall. I held onto the sink and cried with all of my heart. *This might be it. Oh God, please, NO! Don't take my Daddy. He's such a good man. God, will you help bring him through this surgery?*

It took a while to compose myself, but when I finally was able to do so, I walked back into Dad's ICU room and felt a little stronger. I went over to Mom to explain the situation in a way she could understand. She stood at my father's bedside, holding his hand, and brushing the hair from his forehead. They seemed to have their own special language together. My heart burst full of love watching them.

A little later I headed to the small hospital chapel: A room to reflect; a room for prayer and feeling God's presence. The lights were low; only two small candles were lit on the small altar. A huge old Bible lay opened. Several wooden pews sat closely together and the scent of candle wax permeated the air: a kind-of nostalgic, comforting scent, bringing me back to the many times I attended church with my father. I closed my eyes. There was no need for words because God knew my heart. Calmness descended over me, and loving arms wrapped about me. Though I had thought I couldn't go on earlier that day, I stood and walked from the room to face whatever outcome my father's surgery would bring that evening.

Later that night, before he was wheeled away for surgery, Dad had a special word for each of us. To me he said, "Thanks for everything, Honey. Don't let your mother keep the heat too high in the house." Oh Dad . . .

My son was away on an out-of-state trip at the time. Rick and I called a few friends to ask if they would wait with us during the time of the surgery. After taking my mother to the cafeteria to eat a little, we all met in the waiting room near ICU.

The tight band of tension never left my stomach. It was as if a knot kept tightening and loosening and then leaving an empty hole in its place; a hole that felt like it would never heal.

Anything could happen. Dad could die right on the surgery table. It could be a success or failure. None of us knew. Mom was seated in a wheelchair because I'd known it would be too much for her to walk. She started singing little nonsense songs and it broke a little of the tension.

A few hours later, the female doctor came into the room. The look on her face was not of sorrow. "Well, he made it through surgery," she said. "He'll be in intensive care for a while. Now we wait and see." She shook hands all around. "A nurse will be out for you when he's back in the room. Have a good night." The doctor left. She looked exhausted. It was around nine p.m.

When the family was able to see Dad, his body was filled with tubes and wires. He was not awake, but every one of us took a turn to give good wishes. I couldn't believe my brave father had made it through one more time.

~

Dad's condition went up and down. When they first took him off the ventilator and he could breathe on his own, I thanked God that this strong man was going to be okay. It seemed that Dad had nine lives like a cat. I couldn't believe how good he looked.

Things weren't stable for long though. Dad had setbacks and his oxygen levels faltered. He was intubated again and kept sedated. I visited my father early in the day through the next couple of weeks and I watched numbers on his screens. Though I wanted him to know that I was there, I didn't want him to fight the ventilator. It broke me to watch him that way. I took Mom occasionally, but by this time, we weren't sure what the outcome might be.

I worried constantly about my mother being home. Though she managed pretty well, and Rick was with her through the night, I spent so much time on the phone with her when I drove home each evening. Did she take her pills? Could I really trust that she was telling me the truth? Had she eaten? My mother wouldn't come to stay with me. She had a dog and three cats that needed her, she said. She would be fine.

~

Blip, bleep went the hospital monitors and the whoosh of the ventilator—the most hated and loved of life-saving devices. Drip drop went intravenous fluids. Sometimes Dad drifted in and out of sleep when they took his medication down a notch. His eyes opened for a moment and he waved to a few of us who'd gathered at his bedside.

Each one of us took turns to whisper words of encouragement. Matt told Lamp that his YouTube fans were sending their prayers and good wishes. Dad smiled. I knew it was a smile, for I saw those eyes twinkle. He'd been so proud of being in one of my son's YouTube videos playing games in an arcade and winning a Betty Boop doll. Several of the kids liked Dad so much they asked for his autograph.

My mother laid her head against his arm. Their fingers were entwined together. Sixty years. A good marriage. I showed the nurses pictures on my cell phone of Mom and Dad when they first wed; those two gorgeous people in their early lives with so much hope before them.

I prayed out loud offering words of comfort and strength. Dad closed his eyes. He prayed in his own way.

All the silly names he called us through the years floated through my mind and the nonsense language he invented. How I wanted to hear those words from his lips right then. He wanted to talk the day before. I filled in the blanks for him as I watched his eyes and hands. I tried my best to envision what he wanted to tell us all.

As I stood there, more memories came unbidden: the silly hats Dad used to put on when we went shopping together. Once he donned a type of fedora and pretended to be Hannibal Lector from *Silence of the Lambs*. A big tin popcorn can went onto his head one Christmas as he breathed like Darth Vader stating, "Luke, I am your father." He unzipped his postal sweater one evening after work singing "It's a Beautiful Day in the Neighborhood" as well as Fred Rogers.

All of the movies he loved best played through my head in succession: Peter Sellers in the Inspector Clouseau movies, *Marathon Man* with Dustin Hoffman, *Gone with The Wind* and all the war pictures he loved. We watched them so many times we were able to quote whole scenes from some of them.

I thought of our favorite song, "The Emperor Waltz." I'd bought my father a CD and he blasted that piece of music loudly whenever he worked on crafts. I wish we'd have danced to it together just once.

A good life, a good man. Even the nurses told us that. When they asked how he felt, they always got a "thumbs up" from Dad. From the little they knew of our family story and the times they were able to actually speak with him, every person who met Dad in the hospital said the same thing: What a good guy.

The last time I saw my father in a regular room, he was agitated. He wasn't doing well and the doctors said that he most likely already had sepsis in his system. Who do you blame? Do you get angry because they should have done the surgery right away? We knew how strong our father was. No matter what percentage his heart had been, he most likely would have made it through surgery if it had been done immediately. He may not have gone septic, but who knows?

I thought back to how uncomfortable he'd said his stomach was all summer. Perhaps events had just been leading up to this all along.

Though I didn't want to say goodbye to my father, a popular Christian song popped into my head. It was called "Thy Will be Done." It was a powerful song that touched me with beautiful words that spoke of letting go and putting trust in God, especially when things seem bleak. Did I have the courage though?

Seated on the large windowsill of the hospital, I stared into the darkened sky watching the stars flicker one by one. He shouldn't have to suffer any longer. Perhaps it was time to let him go. Complete brokenness enveloped me in its gloomy embrace. My heart shattered into fragments. Though it took all the strength I could bear, I said the words right then. *Thy will be done, Lord.*

The next morning I drove back in early to the hospital. I knew what I wanted to say to my father. I had to talk to him even though he was heavily sedated.

The nurses greeted me right away. I could see that Dad was slumped and appeared unconscious. His vital signs did not look good. The nurses said it would be a day of decisions. Dad's body was shutting down little by little. I told them I would call my brother and Mom, but first I asked for a little time alone with him.

I stood beside him looking into the still handsome face. The ventilator whooshed and monitors droned. I did something I'd never done. I laid my head near my father's shoulder. I put my hand on his chest. "Dad," I said, "I want you to know it's okay to let go. Stop fighting and go on to Heaven. We've been so blessed to have you all these years, but now you need to meet your other children that you lost. They're waiting for you.

"I promise to take care of Mom. She will be fine. You've done all you can and fought hard. Now you go to your reward. I love you. Be at peace." Tears streamed down my face, hot rivulets of sadness, but I was determined not to falter.

A little later, Rick brought Mom to the hospital. A few friends and family members showed up to be with us. I watched my mother carefully. I felt that sometimes Alzheimer's can be a blessing.

Dad and His Sister, My Aunt Lil

Dad's Senior Yearbook Photo

Dad in Korea

CHAPTER 34

*W*e had all made the decision to remove life support from Dad. There was nothing else that could be done. I stood looking around at all the people who came to stand with us that day when a shimmery vision caught my eyes. Surrounding my father at the head of his bed, on either side, and at the foot of his bed were four stately beings. It appeared they looked like knights of some sort. Were they angels sent to usher Dad out of this world? I glanced at my brother and his friends. I realized I was the only one who could see them. A sense of awe overwhelmed me. Strength filled me. Peace washed over me. When it was my turn to say my last goodbye to my father, I was able to leave the room without carrying on.

Though a few others stayed behind when they removed the ventilator, my brother and I could not. Rick went home, and I went for a walk outside the hospital. Neither of us felt strong enough to witness our father's last breath.

Because it was early September, there were beautiful flowers planted all around the outside of the hospital. I walked past them as I'd walked with my father at other times, admiring their beauty. I listened to the call of birds in the trees while the sun shone warmly and brightly above. I held onto the vision of the heavenly visitors I'd just witnessed. Just knowing where my father was headed brought me such comfort.

After a few minutes, I headed to a small wooden bench near the side of the hospital. I may have only sat there for a moment or so, but then I looked up to where my father's room was. I heard Dad whisper, "The nightmare is over." Just then my cell phone buzzed. My dear friend Jaci texted: *Where are you? Let me know when you are back up here.*

I texted: *Why, is he gone?*

She texted back: *Yes, just now, very peacefully.*

I smiled as I looked up into the sky. Dad had given me a sentence upon his departure using our special phrase: nightmare. For he'd always said whenever something awful happened: *What a nightmare.* It was also confirmation that my friend texted at the very time Dad had spoken to me. It would be something I held onto as I'd held on to my father's love.

When we gathered at my parent's house later in the day, I wondered what on earth we were going to do with Mom. The hole in my heart was ripped wide open. Not only was Dad gone, but we would have to deal with her Alzheimer's/dementia on our own. My brother and I didn't speak about it right then, but in both of our minds, questions were forming. Mom had gone three weeks without Dad while he was in the hospital and it hadn't been easy. What would the rest of her life mean now? How long would the rest of her life be?

She was surprisingly strong through those days, and it was one of the many times that I would feel again that dementia was a blessing and not a curse. She certainly knew what had happened with Dad, but dementia tempered her emotions somehow. There were times she became childlike and sang silly songs that didn't seem appropriate. Or she spoke about movies she had always loved instead of talking about Dad. This seemed to have all the markings of God's hand imprinted onto it for me.

By mid-fall of 2016, a difficult journey began for me, my brother and son. Mom loved her home and we knew it would be best to keep her there as long as possible.

But then every minute of every day started to become a time of uncertainty. Was Mom eating well? Did she remember her pills? She was alone most of the time and I would call her constantly. "Did you have your breakfast? Can you check your pill container? Does it look like Tuesday's pills are gone?" I couldn't trust the answers she gave me. Worry consumed us all.

Though she knew us, and could still do simple tasks, she forgot so many other normal elements of a routine day. Her television became too complicated. Even her telephone became a mystery. She couldn't hear it ringing. She was unable to dial out on a cordless phone or to hang up after a call, leaving the line open. We turned to other alternatives. A simple old-fashioned princess phone was the answer. Yet it only provided a small respite in one area. I ordered Meals on Wheels for dinnertime, but would see some of them piled in the freezer when I visited. I finally beat that game when I realized I could call local pizza places and have sandwiches delivered to her and also pay for them right over the phone.

We faced daily coordination issues, including her difficulty with phone calls, trying to find someone who could stay with her for an hour or two on a particular day, worries about her sitting all day staring at a blank television screen. Could she make herself coffee, did she feed the animals, did she wet the bed, or has she washed herself? The list was endless so our lives were filled with Mom.

CHAPTER 35

ime slowed to a crawl. My days were consumed with worry over my mother. Though my brother still stayed with her at night, there was nobody there through most of the days. I had a job that I could not quit, and still visited two days or so a week. I enlisted my son to check on Gram. He took her shopping and out to lunch one day a week. Two girlfriends of mine also pitched in to stop over. We were very fortunate to be able to work the situation out for a little while. I tried to enlist the help of a lady from church to care for Mom, but my mother became suspicious and didn't like her.

I called her several times a day from work and panicked if Mom didn't answer. Mostly her television set became the object of frustration for us all. The newer sets had several remote control devices to use: one you had to turn the power on and another to get to the correct input. There was even one more for Mom's DVD movies. I made small signs and taped them on the backs of the controllers. If I was on the phone with my mother and heard television static in the background, I turned her attention to the backs of her remotes. For a while she was able to navigate them. But soon after, she didn't understand how they worked.

I lay awake at four in the morning, totally unable to find that cozy spot once again or to stop the thoughts which pummeled me from all sides. Will Mom be all right today? Will she eat and take her pills? What if she missteps and takes a fall? Is her health okay?

On the days I was with her, I tried to give her my all. I made her a scrumptious breakfast, bacon, French toast and coffee. I did my best Lumiere impression from *Beauty and the Beast* and sang "Be My Guest" as I served her. I loved to make Mom laugh, and it was no easy task to think up a barrage of chatter so she wouldn't go down any of the paths of depression. Dementia was enough without the added sadness she sometimes carried during that time.

I glanced around for tasks that needed done since I wanted to be of help to my brother who already did so much. I washed clothes, took care of the cats, did a light dusting, helped Mom to dress or heaven forbid, take a shower. For that was not easy and on the days I was able to coax her, I ended up getting almost as wet as she did. I knew she felt badly. It couldn't be easy having your daughter insist you do some-thing that had become scary. The tub was not easy to maneuver with the bad hip she'd had most of her life, and getting her onto her shower seat took patience and a little muscle as well.

Some days I took Mom for the drive to her favorite spot near that lovely creek and small stone bridge. We grabbed a little food when we were out, but taking a walker in and out of the car and making sure she didn't fall, gave every trip a little added stress.

I orchestrated all her doctor, dental, eye and foot appointments like a well-oiled machine, seeing that she was cared for. And getting her to them was another feat in itself.

Once she was situated back home, I made sure that Mom took her late afternoon pills; or days when I wasn't there, tried talking her into taking them on the other end of the phone. It was exhausting, these simple tasks, and sometimes as part caregiver, I wanted to vent and scream and even run away.

My friend Goldie reminded me to care for myself. It had been easy to fall into a trap--an endless pit of despair at times. Poor me, why me, etc, etc. But when I actually listened to Goldie, my spirits lifted and the shackles of depression began to abate. I saw a movie by myself. I took time to read good books, listen to music I enjoyed, and on occasion, even painted my nails with glitzy, fun colors. My husband was so kind to me during this time; he knew what it was like to be close to parents. Several years ago, he'd lost both of his parents within eight months of each another.

~

Mom had a Facebook account and began accusing friends and family of avoiding or ignoring her. She told me that nobody sent her any condolences about Dad's passing. We tried to tell her that she missed the posts, but she wouldn't hear of it. Things got to the point where she didn't remember much each day. She told me she hadn't seen my brother, and then told him I never called or came around anymore. We both knew the truth though. No matter how much we gave of ourselves, dementia erased every deed.

I noticed that my mother was wearing the same clothes when I visited. She went to sleep in them and kept them on for days. This was so unlike the clean lady she used to be.

We began to do small sink baths instead of showers. I was hurting for all the changes in her, and I couldn't believe I was dressing her like a child. Thoughts threatened to creep in about her mental illness, but I kept them at bay. I prayed them away. "This is not the same," I said.

~

All of our firsts without Dad were unbearable. Thanksgiving and Christmas felt empty. Though my brother and I kept things as light as possible for Mom, our hearts weren't truly in it and our grief, so fresh.

Right after Christmas, Mom landed in the hospital for gastrointestinal bleeding once again. She was terrified as I reached her bedside in the emergency department of Heritage Valley. I'd spend so many days with my father at this same hospital and here I was with my remaining parent. Would there never be an end to the health issues and sad events in our lives?

She looked so small in the bed and her eyes sought mine for comfort and words of encouragement. I played my role well.

"You look good," I said. "Your numbers are great. I think you are having a bout of bad diarrhea, that's all."

Mom seemed a bit calmer with my words. Yet she was still bleeding quite regularly and was admitted to the hospital for more tests.

I knew this time would be much more difficult for her. The dementia was worsening, and I feared leaving her. She would never understand where she was or why she was there. I stayed late every single night as the nurses reassured me that she was in good hands. Though she could have succumbed to the blood loss, Mom made it through this time and was sent to a rehab facility next. There was no way she could go home, the doctors said.

Mom's time at the rehab facility went better than expected. She was all smiles and very pleasant to the aides and nurses. People there grew to really like her in the few weeks of her visit. She did her rehabilitation exercises like a pro. Even a few of the little memory games went some-what well and I felt hopeful. Until the day she asked about my son.

"Kar," Mom said, sitting in her wheelchair with lunch before her. "Now, Matt . . .Who's son is he?"

I gulped. Oh no. Not her grandson. How could she not know that he's mine?

"He's my son, Mom," I said.

"Oh yeah," she replied and went on eating.

We took her home at the end of her stay, and she seemed to be stable for a while.

CHAPTER 36

*T*he red cardinal had stayed nearby through the winter months. His glorious color stood out against the brilliant white snow covered branches. Now it was approaching March and he was never very far when I went outdoors. Sometimes he brought the missus with him, but more often than not, he visited alone. I began to think of him as my friend; a comforter that showed me beauty in the times that seemed so dark otherwise. I began to place seeds in my open palm and call out to him. Though he watched me closely from a nearby branch, and his little head turned this way and that, he wouldn't breach the gap between human and bird.

I thought about the way some people thought of cardinals as signs. I asked for a sign for my mother. I wondered how to pray for her.

Signs popped up in our town, literally, for the local high school production of *Beauty and the Beast*. It was set for mid March, so I had several weeks to plan our excursion. It had always been one of Mom's favorite Disney movies, one she watched over and over with my son when he was little. I knew she would enjoy this play and I began telling her about it every chance that I could.

The day arrived. I couldn't contain my excitement. Mom would love this! It would be exactly what she needed—a little time out, familiar songs that she knew, something totally different from her everyday life. She would be around other people, and she'd thank me for it when it was all over.

I got to her house, and though I'd told her for days and weeks about it, she had no idea where we were going. I explained that my son and I were taking her to a high school production of one of her favorite movies.

On the drive, she seemed fine. Fine, that was, until we got out of the car. Mom complained about the weather—it was way too cold. The wind whipped at us as we trudged what felt like miles into the school. What if she had to use the bathroom? Why did the auditorium have to be so far away? What if she wasn't comfortable in the seats? The list went on and on. People looked at us as I tried hurrying her along; her voice raised decibels above the usual.

I had a really bad moment and finally snapped. Lashing out I said, "Fine, if you're going to be like this, let's turn around and go home." I meant it. All my planning for a perfect day shot down with her negativity. I couldn't remember her dementia in that moment. All I could think about was me.

When the lights finally dimmed in the auditorium, Mom innocently asked, "Is this *Cats*?" It was a question she would repeat at least twenty-five times.

Mom began to sing along quite loudly with the songs she knew from the play. I wanted to disappear into my seat, and wondered what the people sitting near us thought about her.

A little later, I began to relax a bit, thinking that she was finally beginning to enjoy herself, but then she exclaimed, "I want to see *Cats!*" My stress level went through the roof. I thought about getting up and leaving with her. Part of me wanted to sneak off and pretend I didn't know her. Something inside me, however said: *Stay until the end. This is a day for her to enjoy. Don't worry if she's embarrassing you.* After that I silently dared anyone sitting near us to complain about her.

When the play was over, tears poured down Mom's face. The Beast is dying, and Belle's love saves him. It was a tale she'd told me many times when I was younger. In this moment, I saw something with perfect clarity: My mom was now like a little child.

We walked out of the auditorium and spotted the lovely star of the show posing for pictures with excited little girls. Mom shyly asked me, "Can I have a picture with Belle?" My heart cracked into two. That child again showed up through the wrinkled skin, thinning hair, missing teeth and lost memories.

"Of course," I said, and we snapped away at a few poses. Mom beamed like a little girl, one who believed in magic, beauty and love. Who was I to take that from her?

Mom Posing with Belle from "Beauty and the Beast."

CHAPTER 37

The day after the school play, Jim and I were off work together. We had a ten o'clock appointment with our tax man that morning. My brother called early.

"Kar, something weird happened," he said. "Mom fell earlier this morning in the bathroom."

Oh no, I thought. Now what?

"She was talking a little weird, not making sense. She asked me for a sandwich while she was on the floor. I got her up though and she's in the living room sitting on the couch. She wasn't hurt from the fall."

I asked if she was making more sense now. Thoughts of a urinary tract infection swept through my mind. I knew when the elderly had them that they sometimes acted very odd. Jim's uncle who I'd helped while in a nursing home had the infections constantly and it sounded like that to me.

"Call her doctor," I suggested. There was no way I could drop what I was doing at that moment to go in. I convinced myself that it was indeed a UTI and would check back with them after our morning appointment. If the doctor would see her today, we could pick her up around noon or so.

However, it was not a urinary infection. Mom landed in the

hospital once again due to her odd symptoms. She was not able to walk well without aid, and she spoke in very quiet, hushed tones if at all. Upon examining her, it was found that she had what was called Lacunar Infarct strokes. These affect walking and speaking, and also cause more confusion. I thought of what my dad used to always say about Mom, "Poor girl," he'd said. She'd had her share of difficulties and now we were dealing with a series of strokes on top of it all.

She had one particularly bad episode while in the hospital when the nurses were bringing her back to bed after going to the bathroom. She slackened and became unconscious. I was on the phone with my brother when I saw extra nurses running into the room and heard a buzzer sounding. "Oh my gosh!" I screamed. "Something's wrong with Mom!"

Poor Rick hung up as I waited to see what would come of this episode. After scrambling a few minutes, Mom was back. Crisis was averted for the time. I called my brother back immediately to let him know she was okay.

After a short hospital stay, Mom was transferred back to the rehab facility she'd been to before. This time wasn't the same though. She hardly seemed able to do the rehabilitation. She tired so easily. She barely spoke. Mostly, she slept almost all the time. I sat in her room days on end with a crocheting project I was working on. I ended up calling it The Memory Blanket because it was during the worst of Mom's time with her memory, and it helped me to remember the good.

As my fingers worked at the yarn, I began to think about all the years gone by. From time to time I would glance at my mother. She appeared peaceful in her dozing. Occasionally she would mumble as if talking with someone. Was it Dad? Was he perhaps humming "their" song to her? *No arms could ever hold you like these arms of mine . . .*

I thought back to the cute story of how my parents met. Their families had known one another in our small town. Since Dad was almost six years older, they had never really looked at each other in any special way. It wasn't until after the Korean War when my father came

139

back in uniform to Ambridge. He'd been an ambulance driver in Korea.

Eileen (my mother) was in the old Buick with her cousin Walter who knew Richie (my dad) really well. Richie was standing at the corner in front of Enelow's Shoes, on Merchant Street where all of our stores were located in town. He was wearing his army uniform. Walter rolled down his window and beeped, waving wildly at his old friend. Mom asked her cousin, "Walt, who is that?" It was clear that she found the young soldier very attractive.

"That's Rich Mattia," Walter said. "He's back from the army." Walter saw something in his cousin's face. "I'll re-introduce you to him."

When Eileen and Rich finally met, they could hardly believe they had known one another in their earlier years. Eileen was only eighteen-years-old at the time. The shy, polite, handsome man was everything she'd dreamed about.

Rich's heart was taken with the long-haired beauty with the sensuous blue eyes. Though she was prim and proper, he felt himself longing for her love. A quick courtship led to marriage when Eileen turned nineteen.

From all the photos I'd seen of their early life together and the beautiful cards and notes Dad wrote, I realized my parents' love was very special. A once-in-a-lifetime type of love.

CHAPTER 38

*N*ow Rick and I were faced with the daunting task of searching for a good care facility for Mom. There was no way she could go back to her home any longer. She needed constant care; she was incontinent and unable to walk without aid. Mostly she was wheelchair-bound, and still she slept and slept.

We were very fortunate to find a lovely place in Patterson Heights that had an elegant dining area, very clean rooms, and sweet staff. We set to work making her space as comfortable and cozy for Mom as possible.

We brought Mom a radio/CD player and some of her favorite music. We brought decorations from home that held special meaning, her favorite blankets, and a dry erase board where we left loving messages to her. Rick brought my mother the special doll he'd gotten her for Christmas a few years back. That original doll held quite a story. Mom told us once about a fond Christmas remembrance from when she was a child:

I was born into a family who had lived through the great depression. We were poor in the 1930's and 1940's and Christmas gifts were the last things our parents cared about. Yet one year, an elderly man who lived near us took it upon himself to bestow one of the best Christmas gifts I'd ever received.

We children often got small gifts of fruits and nuts in a stocking, but one Christmas a gentleman knocked on the door of our small apartment. He handed my mother a tissue-wrapped package. "For the little girl," he'd said, coat buttoned against the cold, frosty breath blowing before him as he stood on the stoop.

Nobody knew why he'd chosen to bring this one special gift to a little girl he barely knew, but when I opened the package, a beautiful dolly peeped out at me. Brown curly hair, blue snowsuit with fur trim. I saw something I'd only dreamed about.

The cherished doll was priceless to me, something to love and hold near when my drunken father spouted abusive words. The doll was my strength and belief that kindness existed.

Years later, my most prized gift vanished when our family moved into a new house. I walked past the old apartment I used to live in, trying to peek through a window to see if the doll was still there. I never saw it again.

One Christmas a couple years ago, as Mom opened her last gift, her face crinkled into a frown. My brother and son sat close by watching her carefully. What was up, I wondered?

She peeled layers of tissue paper from the box and then began to cry. There, before her was a doll, much like the one of her youth. My brother had found one just like it. Years melted away and the little girl untouched by sadness and grief once again shone like the sun.

As they wheeled Mom into her new room, words couldn't describe the feeling in my chest—of my heart splintering into tiny fragments, each one burnished with good and bad memories alike. Only three short weeks ago we were able to take her out to eat and go on drives. Three short weeks ago we saw the play at the high school, and Mom sang along to the Disney tunes she knew and loved so well.

I saw a woman before me whom I barely recognized; she was almost completely devoid of any emotion. Gone was the laugh that was so cute. Gone were the stories told over and over, stories we all knew better than her but listened patiently as they were told.

Her eyes held a tiny spark of light when she looked at me, Rick, or

Matt. I would have given anything to see life rejuvenated in her, or something that would fill her with emotions once again.

My brother handed Mom the beautiful dolly he'd given her for Christmas a short time ago. She sat in her wheelchair, stroking the dolly, covering it with the blanket that lay around her own shoulders. My eyes filled with tears and it was difficult to remain stoic. I stayed with her until much later in the day, watching old movies, trying to get her to eat in the dining room with new friends, seeing if talk of cooking and baking would bring her around just a little.

I left later that night feeling a tight band around the upper part of my stomach; the band of fear and uncertainty. I knew it well, for it was with me when my father had been in the hospital—a hated, familiar companion formed by tension and worry.

I couldn't find my laughter and didn't enjoy much. My work days were filled with stress and I didn't like who I had become—someone who snapped in anger over situations I used to handle much better. Most of my thoughts were of Mom and wondering how she was and wishing I could be with her.

I'd read about others who went through this before me. I saw pictures of smiling faces and realized that life did return, and there would be rainbows and sunshine again. This was a season in my family's journey about two parents both so loved. My brother and I would hold onto what we had with our mother until her own story ended. Then we would have to make new memories and remember with fondness the old ones so lovingly tucked away in our hearts.

Mom and the Christmas Doll

Mom Cuddling her Doll

CHAPTER 39

*U*nfortunately our time was short at the Patterson Township care home. It had something to do with finances, and we had to move Mom once again. It hurt to think about taking her to another place because I'd seen a few glimmers of hope: she played a little Bingo with me and a few ladies one day; she tried to make some of the little crafts they taught; and she ate with gusto a plate of pasta I'd made her. Such good signs. I prayed that perhaps we could move her to my town and then I would be able to see her every single day. That didn't work out, and it was probably for the best. Mom would have been too far away from some of the others who visited. She was transferred to another place in Hopewell Township, a very small but friendly facility.

At first, Mom seemed more sad and depressed than usual. When one of the staff tried to give her a shower, she told me that my mother had cried the whole time. I asked if they would please just do sponge baths in bed. I knew that she hated to be cold and uncomfortable and showers must have felt like torture to her.

Also, Mom had C-Dif, a bacterial infection of the colon which caused chronic, infectious diarrhea and had to be handled carefully. It made me sad because I knew that she needed human touch now more than ever. Yet when I was around her, I wore gloves to cut her nails or brush her hair gently.

I arrived early one morning at the care facility as one of the nurses was bathing and dressing Mom in bed. It appeared my mother had enough. She began to sob deep, heart-wrenching cries that broke my heart. It may have been the pain of her arthritis, but I did something uncharacteristic and hugged her around the shoulders and stroked her back gently reciting words of love and comfort. The nurse stood back and let me do what only a family member could. Mom cried and I soothed. I held onto her and kissed the top of her head tenderly. I noticed a pretty bracelet on her arm and began to talk about it. I pointed out the butterfly ring she always wore. Like a small child, Mom's tears subsided into sniffles as she concentrated on her pieces of jewelry. I sat back content that a crisis had been averted, and thanked God for giving me the tenderness needed in that moment even though I had never done this before with her.

In the dining area, I sat with my mother while she ate. She always fell asleep in the wheelchair afterward, and I sat with her taking in the rise and fall of her chest, her sweet, closed eyes, and every little nuance I could. I thought about that voice that I'd heard on my porch swing about enjoying time with my mother. I realized it had foretold of her Alzheimer's/dementia. Though I lost my mom already in many ways, I truly took in every precious second and breath.

I sometimes wheeled my mother around outside while we listened to the chirping of the birds in the trees and enjoyed the warmth of sunny days. I told her stories about the birds, the butterflies floating nearby in the little garden of flowers, and the cute dog that was a part of weekend visits there. I thought about all the little stories she'd made up through the years. I had taken over that sweet duty.

When we went back inside for her lunch, I sat content by her side, enjoying the time with my quiet mother and learning all the different oddities of the others seated around her.

There was a man who wheeled himself around and around the room as if searching for his lost love. There was a boisterous lady who reminded us of an old family friend with a biting, sarcastic humor. There was a sweet black lady who was blind, and had a marvelous singing voice and a huge sweet tooth for candy. A Korean lady befriended me and tried to get Mom to talk more. These people had become a normal part of my life. I'd grown fond of them, and looked forward to seeing them when I visited my mother.

How was I to know that in three months my mother would be gone? How do any of us ever know? No, her health wasn't great, but she seemed stable. It had been easy to picture heading into autumn and Halloween at the facility, and then Thanksgiving and Christmas. In my mind I planned all sorts of fun things for Mom and the other residents. I would read stories to them, and make little gift bags. I couldn't wait.

Friday of the first week in July of 2017, I got a very serious phone call from the Home. Mom began bleeding, vomiting blood actually. They wanted to know my choice of hospital for her. I chose the older hospital that we had used most of our lives; they knew her history best, and would give her good care. I phoned my work office and told them I wouldn't be in because my mother had another emergency.

By the time I got to the emergency room, Mom was doing better, rather quiet and calm. A doctor pulled me aside and much like our decision with Dad, told me it may be time to let the Good Lord intervene if He so chose. She had lost huge amounts of blood. They would only give her a blood transfusion if the family requested it, but in observing her failing health, her passing would be inevitable anyway. My brother and I spoke about it, and as long as Mom was comfortable and not vomiting any longer (they had given her something for that), we would begin the vigil of letting her go.

Though she hadn't been speaking much, as I stood near Mom, she said very clearly, "Bible." I thought it was odd, but I asked her if she saw one. She nodded. She also mumbled something about seeing people. I wondered just what she saw that we did not. The hospital released Mom back to her care facility. It would be there we would begin the wait.

I remember sitting with my mother back at the care facility later that day. She touched the jacket I wore and said, "Pretty."She fell asleep, became agitated, and then awoke pulling at her covers. I reassured her with words of comfort and sat by her side quietly for hours.

One thing that was odd: I brought up the name Claude Palmer to my mother, the fellow we had known so well from her days at the Eight Street Dairy. We had recently found one another again on Facebook. I wondered if she would remember him. With a serene look on her face my mother smiled and said, "Claude Palmer." She remembered.

The next day my husband and I visited with Mom. She did not wake up. Her breathing was shallow and the gurgle in her chest had begun. I laid my head upon my mother's shoulder while tears found their way out of the corners of my eyes. I began singing softly to my mother, songs she'd sung to comfort me as a child. Later that night, I received a phone call around three a.m. Mom wouldn't be here much longer. I lived an hour away and wanted to leave immediately. My husband was worried for me driving at that hour and in the state I was in. My brother was able to be at our mother's side, and we remained on the phone together for a long while.

My brother later told me that a sound like soft footsteps seemed to enter the room but no nurse was there. A napkin blew down from Mom's table, but no breeze created it. And in our mother's hands was clutched her Miraculous Medal necklace, but we couldn't imagine how it had gotten there. Mom passed very peacefully.

I remember being strong for myself and other family members during the preparations for her funeral. I remember holding up well and greeting loved ones and friends with my own comfort for them and the words, "I know she is with God and Dad now." And my mother looked beautiful--radiant almost. I had no difficulty standing near her casket and soaking in every last detail that I could of her.

I have many emotions when I think back on all that our family has gone through in these last few years. Two years of losing both parents. Two years of Mom's dementia and failing health. Part of what I feel is guilt. Guilt over relief that a burden has been lifted. Guilt over not being there for my mother's final breath. Guilt over making the decision about the blood transfusion. But what is it that Mom always said?

My mother wrote me many notes and little letters in cards through the years. And one that I found recently said this: *All our love always and forever. I want you to know all bad things pass but good thoughts last forever. Hold those good thoughts in your heart.*

And another: *My Dearest Karen, I'm not the writer you are, but I speak from my heart. We grew together not just mother and daughter, but best friends also. We had laughs over the years but most of all, love. When you tell me I taught you compassion, you already had it when I was sick in your early years. I have been proud to be your mother. We are human, Kar, the Lord didn't mean for us to be angels on this earth. To me being kind and sympathetic as we all are is what I believe the Lord wanted for us. Don't waste this precious life on past mistakes; live it with joy and laughter as much as possible. All my love, Mom*

These tangible reminders of how my mother saw life are guides--beacons to me--of how she wants me to live. Would she want me to remain guilt-ridden? I think not. Would she want me to wallow in depression? No. I think Mom is speaking to me through these little notes. I think she always knew how I would feel--how I would take her passing. As always, she is there to teach me and guide me. And in my heart, I know that these feelings will pass.

Weeping may endure for a night, but joy comes in the morning. Psalm 30:5 (And in the mourning.)

Me and Mom at Christmas

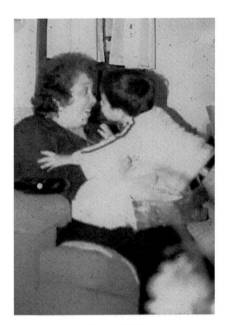

Mom and Rick

Mom When She Was a Little Girl

School-age Mom

CHAPTER 40

O ne day at the dental office where I work, I saw an elderly dementia patient clutching her little bag of freebies as if they were the greatest thing she ever received. Even when her daughter tried to take the bag from her, she held it closely, because to her, they were her possessions. She may not have much left in her memories, but at that moment, those little dental "gifts" became the most important thing to her. A lump formed in my throat, and a few tears sprang to my eyes. How that reminded me of my mother.

I thought back to the time when Mom still lived in her own home. When all of us tried to do our very best to make sure she ate, kept up with doctor visits, and to be sure she wasn't alone very long. She may have lost many of her memories, but she had small routines that meant something to her. She fed and cared for her cats. She pulled her driver's license out of her purse and her health insurance card and read them many times. She read the small love notes from my father time and again. How we rolled our eyes when she would begin these routines, never realizing how important they were to her, and how in small ways, they were keeping her memory going.

It may have been one of the most difficult times in our family, but we had the strength to go through it. It exhausts me to think about it now, but when we needed it, God supplied exactly enough of His mercy and grace to us all.

Now that Mom is gone almost three years, I miss those little nuances of hers. What I wouldn't give to hear her stories again.

Halloween was tough for me without Mom because it was a holiday she had enjoyed so much. At Thanksgiving I couldn't help but think that even though it wasn't my favorite holiday, it was one of hers. How Mom loved her kitchen. The fact that she'd begin baking days in advance, planning her usual feast, and having it all turn out perfectly. A few years ago, even with Alzheimer's, she managed somehow. But her last year was different, and she allowed us to take her to a restaurant that day. I like to think she still enjoyed herself with her family surrounding her because she smiled through the entire meal.

When the first Christmas without Mom approached with colorful decorations everywhere, joyous songs and yearly traditions, I felt blue. I knew I was not the same person I'd been. I didn't feel the need to make dozens of lists: of cookies, shopping, cleaning and planning. That year, time meant more to me than ever. The time I spent with our children, my brother and family, and dear friends. I did not overdo my spending, for I was more thoughtful. There was no quota to meet, no amount more precious than a kind word to a loved one, and thankfulness for all the blessings in our families.

I had to remember to be kind to myself. I lost two parents in the span of nine months, and I didn't feel like celebrating that holiday season. I was quieter than usual, a little less festive. I didn't place every single decoration that I had from years past. And that was okay. I gave myself the gift of time; time to grieve and remember, time to reflect, but mostly the time to heal.

I also approached the New Year with trepidation. In my mind, all I could picture was the fact that neither of my parents had made it to 2018. It would be the first full year that they weren't around at all together or apart. I grieved for all that was lost. But then I began to look way back, to a time when I was a little girl. I thought about the days leading up to New Years, and how special they had always been.

I remember when I was little, in the week between Christmas and New Years, Mom always placed a festive tablecloth over our table.

There were cut glass bowls of fruit, silver trays filled with nuts in their shells, and the nut-cracking implements off to the side. There were Torrones, the little Italian boxes piled high on a plate, dried figs, and scads of her homemade cookies on a tiered metal holder.

In our fireplace, colorful, discarded wrapping paper was waiting for the fire that my father would soon build. My toys lay scattered under the tree, a mix mash of dollies, games, and other assorted items, blending in with the manger set: the holy family, wise men and camels.

Our large picture window was painstakingly hand-painted by my father, adorned with all the wonderful sentiments of the season. Through it, I watched the falling snow, the passersby, and my cousins as they filed out of their cars so they could play with (and sometimes break) my new toys.

Aunts, uncles, cousins and grandparents would visit during this most festive time. Talk was lively and loud. Everyone tried to outdo one another with gift-giving tales, stories of food, and memories of their own youth. We also ventured to the homes of other relatives.

New Years Eve would arrive, and though my parents were not drinkers, it was the one time, perhaps, that I would see each of them with a tiny glass of wine to toast the New Year. I was given a glass of ginger ale. The song Auld Lang Syne always brought a lump to my throat even then.

As the years passed, the special holiday week leading up to the New Year was filled with new memories after my brother arrived. Then marriage would follow for me a few years later, and then my own child. I sit wondering where the time has gone for it feels like yesterday that I was the child.

With fresh hopes and dreams in mind, we each face the ticking clock, the countdown of the crystal ball on Times Square. Auld Lang Syne still will bring a tear to some of our eyes, and we, too, will become the memory for our own children and grandchildren.

A good friend had this to say when I told her how sad I felt about my parents not seeing the New Year: *Your parents were such love birds. Just think. They will never have to begin another year separated from one another.*

~

Though sometimes I feel our family went to hell and back, we had glimpses of Heaven through it all. Grief and difficult situations have built character. They haven't swept over us leaving us crippled with doubt and fear. They helped us to see what is really important. When we looked for the small moments of goodness through the pain, when we saw those who touched our lives and showed us that we didn't have to walk the journey alone, we knew that we were not the same people we once were. We have been refined like precious gold, no longer tarnished by the chains that bound us.

When the priest asked what my best memory of my mother was at the blessing service for her at the funeral home, it didn't take me long to recall one for it was recent: "Being caregiver for her journey with Alzheimer's," I'd said.

What does one say to a lifetime of love and memories? How can a person choose their absolute best moment with a beloved parent?

Like snippets of a movie, years worth of laughter, tears, joy and fears played before me. I remembered Mom standing by during my surgery for scoliosis as a teen. She'd been my rock and strength.

When divorce reared its ugly head in my early twenties, my mother was there to rescue me. When fat, ugly tears fell from my eyes and the lies kept surfacing that I wasn't good enough for him and never would be, Mom helped me feel worthy again.

Moments of giggling together like school girls surfaced and drew me in once again and I warmed from the glow. Times of celebration and holidays, the birth of my son, her first grandchild. So many wonderful memories.

Why are those memories the dearest ones that my brother and I hold now? The answer is simple. We got to experience unconditional love given back to a woman who had once loved us the same way.

When a parent has Alzheimer's or dementia-related issues, it is never easy. You wonder if you are the one losing your mind at first. For the questions begin and things are forgotten, appointments are missed, and everything seems upside down.

Then the anger sets in. And for all of us, it is a time of great guilt.

When you find yourself snapping at your elderly parent and watch the hurt in their eyes, the words practically hanging in the air, you wish you could pull them back, place them into a locked box never to surface again. But they do. Just when you feel strong, confident and a little cocky, a challenge arises and you fail. You ask forgiveness and you fail again. There's the maddening cycle--the new normal. Why couldn't they have kept their wits about them to the end?

But then you see them in the most innocent of ways: thinning hair, gummy, lost-tooth smiles. Skin stretched too tightly over prominent bones. You hear whispered words and the innocence of a child, and you realize in their mind, that is where they are. It's all this and more, and you fall deeply in love with your aging parent more than you ever did before. They rely on you, they trust you, and you begin to know that you will never betray that trust.

You also see wise, knowing eyes and the laugh-lined wrinkles around them from years of laughter. You hold onto a hand that worked hard at putting food on the table. You lay your head against their frail chest and listen to the beating of their heart--wondering just how long it will continue . . .

You look at them and see inner beauty shining. No longer a body with a soul, they are now becoming a soul with a body. True loveliness as God intended, no longer superficiality.

Mostly, you give. You give selflessly and totally, turning your emotions and your loved one over to God. You find that He adores them and you, and we are the apple of His eye. He has all of our best interests at the center of His heart. Even if He chooses to take them home, how can we question that glorious time?

Yes, this time can be our best moments and our best memories. With God it is truly possible. Forgiveness, mercy and grace . . . all ours for the taking.

Last summer I was sitting at the table on my back porch with my laptop and a glass of iced tea. Sunshine sparkled off the bird bath and a slight breeze blew behind me tickling the hair against my neck. I heard the loud chirp of a cardinal and looked up to an amazing sight. At the edge of my porch, the red cardinal stood with three fuzzy-headed brown babies in tow. It was such a precious moment, as if he brought them for me to meet.

"What pretty babies," I said. "Thank you for bringing them."

He chirped in answer it seemed.

I told him how happy I've been that he was with me the last three years. I thanked him for his sweetness which gave me something to look forward to each day. I didn't know it at the time but it he was telling me goodbye. I did not see him after that. I have no doubt that he was my beautiful sign and gift of hope from God during a time when I needed it most.

I've developed a heart like my mother, I thought.

One of Mom's favorite phrases was "Everyone has a story." The fact that she could always find a little good in everyone and empathize with others was a lesson she taught us all of her life.

I'd like to think Mom and Dad's story continues in me, my brother, and son. Though I once said that I would never be like her, I now embrace every part of what she left behind in me. I hear her singing "I love you a bushel and a peck." And I know she does.

The End.

Final thoughts . . .

Where Have They Gone? (A Poem by Karen)
A child full of wonder sits on my knee,
and asks, "Where have they gone, where can gram and pap be?"
I hug her and smile, knowing just what to say,
"It isn't the same, but they're not far away.
Heaven's for real, and they're with God you see,
and someday we'll be with them all, you and me."
Her eyes become drowsy; a smile on her face,
She says, "I bet that Heaven's a really nice place."
I sit back content and pray God would start

planting seeds of His love right there in her heart.
She drifts off to sleep, so precious to me,
I whisper a blessing, "Please God let us be . . .
wrapped in your love and your care and your grace;
And let this little one in dreams see your face."
I sigh and remember my own parent's love,
and hope that they watch out for me from above.
Is it possible that heaven can truly be more
than we would have ever imagined before?
If God is this real and He loves us like friends;
Then this isn't over, it's not the end.
If we're like a child and we look for His grace,
will we find it in the simplest place?
My own eyes are closing; I'm drifting to sleep,
I want all good memories to hold and to keep.
When just then I see my dear parents before me,
so handsome and beautiful, wrapped all in glory.
"Yes, heaven's for real," a Voice speaks from above.
"All the tears, all the suffering, are covered by My love.
You'll feel warm and safe; you'll be wrapped in My arms,
with nothing to fear and protection from harm.
Your earthly family is proof that I'm real,
all the good that they've done is something you'll feel.
So carry this back with you upon waking,
My perfect Love is a gift for the taking."
The little one stirs, and her eyes meet mine.
She says, "I want to visit Pap and Gram one more time."
I kiss her small face and I ask, "Did you see them?"
She says "They're so happy, I thought it a dream."
But I know that God has given her a peek;
Of a glimpse of His love like a kiss on her cheek.
And she's got her whole life ahead of her now,
For fun and adventure so I must allow
her own little journey, her own little path,
To take time to giggle and take time to laugh.
The serious things will now have to wait,

I'm praying that her young life will be great.
And hoping that nothing will keep her apart,
of the memories of family and God's loving heart.

Cousins at Christmas With Me

Family Dinner

Mom and Rick's Daughter, Elena

Uncle Lou, Cousin Donna and Family

Me, Matt, and Josh

My Brother Rick and I

Got To Meet My Fourth Grade Teacher Again

Me and Matt